Studies in Major Literary Authors

Edited by

William E. Cain
Professor of English
Wellesley College

A Routledge Series

Studies in Major Literary Authors

William E. Cain, *General Editor*

WRITING "OUT OF ALL THE CAMPS"
J. M. Coetzee's Narratives of Displacement

Laura Wright

Routledge
New York & London

Excerpts from *Waiting for the Barbarians*, *Dusklands*, and *The Life & Times of Michael K*, by J.M. Coetzee, used by permission of Random House Ltd. and Viking Penguin, a division of Penguin Group (USA).

Published in 2006 by
Routledge
Taylor & Francis Group
270 Madison Avenue
New York, NY 10016

Published in Great Britain by
Routledge
Taylor & Francis Group
2 Park Square
Milton Park, Abingdon
Oxon OX14 4RN

10 9 8 7 6 5 4 3 2 1

International Standard Book Number-10: 0-415-97707-X (Hardcover)
International Standard Book Number-13: 978-0-415-97707-4 (Hardcover)

Library of Congress Cataloging-in-Publication Data

Catalog record is available from the Library of Congress

Taylor & Francis Group
is the Academic Division of Informa plc.

Visit the Taylor & Francis Web site at
http://www.taylorandfrancis.com

and the Routledge Web site at
http://www.routledge-ny.com

For Jason

Contents

Acknowledgments

First and foremost, I would like to thank Stephen Clingman for introducing me to J. M. Coetzee, both as a writer and then as a person when he came to the University of Massachusetts in October of 2003 to give the English department's annual Troy Lecture. Thanks also for being such a supportive and dedicated advisor, for taking my opinions and my writing seriously, and for maintaining such a high standard for my work.

I would also like to thank Jenny Spencer for her support of my feminist perspective, for introducing me to the performance theory that has helped to shape this study, and for providing me with a sounding board throughout the writing of this work. Thanks also to Radha Radhakrishnan and Arlene Avakian, for being conscientious readers.

I would like to express my deepest appreciation to my dearest friend, Jamie Davis, whose realistic advice has proven utterly invaluable. Thanks also to Patricia Matthew for inspiring me to write, for pushing me to succeed, and for being such a wonderful mentor and friend. Thanks to Shannon Payne, Bridget Marshall, and Cathy Schlund-Vials for your support and undying humor in the face of some pretty bleak moments.

I would like to thank my parents for their continued faith in me, my father for his optimism and my mother for her genuine interest in my work on Coetzee. Thanks also to my sister and dear friend LeeAnn for always listening to me when I needed someone to listen and for always being able to keep some sense of perspective when I could not.

I would like to thank my partner Jason Sellers whose belief in my abilities and respect for my goals far surpasses anything I ever could have imagined. Thank you for staying with me through this process despite having two cars stolen, having to live through five New England winters, and having to put up with me during the writing of this book.

Finally, I would like to thank William Cain, the editor of the Studies in Major Literary Authors series, for soliciting my work, and Max Novick who acquired my manuscript for Routledge.

Chapter One
(Dis)Placing Coetzee: An Introduction

> The function of criticism is defined by the classic: criticism is that which is duty bound to interrogate the classic. Thus the fear that the classic will not survive the decentering acts of criticism may be turned on its head: rather than being the foe of the classic, criticism, and indeed criticism of the most skeptical kind, may be what the classic uses to define itself and ensure its survival. (J. M. Coetzee, "What is a Classic?: A Lecture," *Stranger Shores* 16)

> One does not, of course, "like" Coetzee. Oily smooth, prickly, repellent, the prose presses, probes, and lets drop the conditions it touches. (Regina Janes, "Writing without Authority" 103)

J. M. Coetzee is an outsider in the realm of white South Africa both as an English speaker with an Afrikaans surname and by virtue of his own self-placement. His writing is continually characterized critically in terms of the things that it and he, by extension, does not do: Coetzee does not express an overt political stance with regard to South Africa in his literature; he does not answer questions after public lectures; he does not write realistic fiction; and now, after a recent move to Adelaide, Australia, Coetzee, as one of South Africa's most prominent writers, does not even live in South Africa. Derek Attridge justifies the absence of explicit ethical action in Coetzee's work claiming that "in both apartheid and post-apartheid society . . . such action is paradoxically undermined by its ideological premises" ("Expecting" 59). Furthermore, just as his work is marked by a refusal to engage publicly in the political realm, Coetzee does not confess details about his personal life as evidenced most explicitly in a recent interview with Eleanor Wachtel in *Brick* during which Coetzee agreed to the discussion under the conditions that

Wachtel ask him no questions about "his own work, his life, or the political situation in South Africa" (38).

How then, one may wonder, is it possible to know Coetzee at all? What sorts of questions does he answer? Of course, Wachtel's interview was all about language, about the choices one makes as a writer with regard to language, in Coetzee's case, a writer who grew up speaking "English at home, Afrikaans in [his] public life" (38) and who writes in English. Such a discussion is, in one sense, merely about language as a literal means of communication, neither about Coetzee's life and his writing, nor about politics in South Africa. But then again, language, especially in the postcolonial, post-apartheid context of Coetzee's works, always gives way to metaphor. In *Boyhood* (1997), the first installment of Coetzee's three-part autobiography, tellingly written in the third person, for example, John makes the unpopular choice of liking the Russians instead of the Americans because of his preference for the letter "r," "particularly the capital *R,* the strongest of all the letters" (27). In *Boyhood,* as in much of Coetzee's writing, the literal—this seemingly aesthetic choice about language—has the symbolic power to place the authorial persona of John outside of acceptable choices. It is from this linguistically determined position as an outsider that Coetzee's ethics begin to become apparent as his authorial choices with regard to language continually make manifest the rhetorical slippage between aesthetic preferences and political representations.

There has been an abundance of criticism leveled at Coetzee for these choices with regard to language and politics, this refusal to realistically represent in his fiction South Africa's political situation as it unfolds before him. For example, Mike Marais describes the acrimony with which *Foe* (1986), Coetzee's metafictional treatment of Daniel Defoe's *Robinson Crusoe,* was met: "while the country was burning, quite literally in some places, the logic went, here was one of our most prominent authors writing about the writing of a somewhat pedestrian eighteenth-century English novelist" ("Death and the Space" 1). But because one cannot read South African literature without reading apartheid, or as Stephen Clingman claims, "in Africa human cannot be separated from historical experience" (*Novels* 3), Coetzee's novels never exclude this historical reality from which they are drawn; instead, Coetzee's rhetorical choices simply deny that there is merely one way to tell *any* story, including the stories of colonization, apartheid, and democracy in South Africa. Coetzee's life, like his writing, has been lived—albeit quietly—in opposition to the master narratives of South African historical experience, and his literary discourse places his work outside of the more traditional periods and themes that have tended to define South Africa's literary history both prior to and since the inception of apartheid in 1948.

* * *

John Maxwell Coetzee was born in Cape Town in 1940, eight years prior to the National Party's political victory and the codification of a long-extant racial oppression under the campaign slogan, "apartheid," or "separateness." According to Michael Green, the 1940s and 50s were characterized by historical fiction written "in response to increasingly militant nationalism" (16). Alan Paton's *Cry the Beloved Country* (1948), for example, was published the same year that the Afrikaner National Party took power in South Africa under the apartheid slogan, yet Paton's narrative resisted, albeit in a sentimental manner, the nationalist racism of such a policy. South Africa's other Nobel Prize winning white writer, Nadine Gordimer, was already writing and publishing short stories in the 1940s. Her second novel, *A World of Strangers,* published in 1958, focuses upon multiracialism, the dominant mode of social and political opposition to apartheid. *Drum* magazine's advent in 1951 provided an outlet for a group of black, predominantly male writers that have since been referred to as epitomizing South Africa's literary renaissance (Driver 231). These writers included editors Lewis Nkosi and Ezekiel Mphahele as well as Alex La Guma, Can Themba, and Bloke Modisane, among others.[1]

Coetzee did not publish his first work of fiction, *Dusklands,* until 1974, but the two extant volumes of his autobiography (or *autrebiography,* as these works are often described by critics like Derek Attridge and Margaret Lenta), *Boyhood* (1997) and *Youth* (2002), situate the protagonist, "John," *within* the context of South African history as an *outsider,* a figure who remains oppositional to the dominant discourse of the 1940s and 50s. John's aforementioned interest in the letter "r" characterizes his generalized *dis*interest in going along with the proverbial crowd and choosing, instead, an internal logic defined by an inherent sense of passionate resistance. For example, in *Boyhood,* the narrator claims, that "he chose [to like] the Russians in 1947 when everyone else was choosing the Americans; having chosen them, he threw himself into reading about them" (27). Furthermore, in the 1960s depicted in *Youth,* John has left South Africa and is living in London, far away from the Sharpeville massacre of 1960 during which police opened fire in a black township and killed 67 demonstrators (Clingman, *Essential* 52). In 1962, the same year that Nelson Mandela was arrested and sentenced to life imprisonment, Alex La Guma, while under house arrest, wrote *A Walk in the Night and Other Stories,* a collection that explores the status of the "colored," or mixed-race, population in a Cape Town slum. By contrast, in *Youth,* John feels that he is free from the political strife that exists in his home country, the strife depicted in La Guma's fiction. His position, for example, is characterized by his ability to exist as an "onlooker" (85) and not an activist at a campaign for nuclear disarmament rally in Trafalgar Square. But the frustration at his own inability to fully escape involvement is apparent when the narrator says,

> out of the frying pan and into the fire! What an irony! Having escaped the Afrikaners who want to press gang him into their army and the blacks who want to drive him into the sea, to find himself on an island that is shortly to be turned to cinders! What kind of world is this in which he lives? Where can one turn to be free of the fury of politics? (85)

Coetzee's representation of the political situation in South Africa is a representation of an authorial desire not to be apolitical, but to exist in self-contained opposition to a political co-opting that is often indicative of active demonstration. Furthermore, mediated through a third-person narrator, the narrative style mimics the narrator's political intention: such an act of displacement complicates any critical ability to define *Boyhood* and *Youth* as typically autobiographical and thereby places these works outside of any one specific literary genre.

In 1970, homeland citizenship was imposed on all Africans, and both the writing and political ideology of the 1970s were characterized by the Black Consciousness Movement, defined by its leader Steve Biko as

> the realisation by the black man of the need to rally together with his brothers around the cause of their operation—the blackness of their skin—and to operate as a group in order to rid themselves of the shackles that bind them to perpetual servitude. It is based on a self-examination, which has ultimately led them to believe that by seeking to run away from themselves and emulate the white man, they are insulting the intelligence of whoever created them black. (49)

The Soweto Revolt of 1976, during which 575 people, mostly schoolchildren, were killed by police forces (Clingman, *Essential* 118), marked a significant moment in Black Consciousness thought. As Stephen Clingman notes, the revolt "was a concerted challenge to the state, and it set the tone for the decade to come. At the same time, however, it was a challenge to white sympathizers" (*Essential* 118). A climate of increasingly violent civil unrest contributed to what Michael Green claims was a skepticism towards the ability to represent the past in fiction (17); *Dusklands,* Coetzee's first work of fiction—which appeared alongside Gordimer's *The Conservationist* (1974) and subsequent to Bessie Head's *A Question of Power* (1973)[2]—exemplifies such skepticism. The second of the two novellas that constitute *Dusklands*, "The Narrative of Jacobus Coetzee," provides a fictional account of eighteenth-century Dutch exploration, and Coetzee's project in this narrative, claims Sheila Collingwood-Whittick, is to expose "to the reader the fraudulent or fictitious nature of documents that feign historical authenticity" ("J. M. Coetzee's" 77). But again Coetzee's work resists a tendency to focus specifically on South Africa; unlike Gordimer and Head whose novels explicitly critique South African history, the first novella of *Dusklands*, "The Vietnam Project," is narrated by an American whose job is to examine the efficacy of psychological warfare during the Vietnam War.

If South African fiction of the 1970s is characterized by a critique of the possibility of truth-telling about the past, literature of the 1980s and early 1990s is perhaps primarily concerned with representing a possible future after the massacres at Sharpeville and Soweto, after the murder of Steve Biko in prison in 1977, and after, as historian Anthony Butler discusses, the removal of 3.5 million people between 1960–1989 as a result of the establishment of so-called ethnic homelands (24). During the 1980s, both Gordimer and Coetzee wrote novels situated in some fictive and potentially apocalyptic future moment. In 1980, the same year that Zimbabwe gained independence, Coetzee wrote *Waiting for the Barbarians*, a novel deeply concerned with its protagonist's inability to imagine a future other than one characterized by the dictates of Empire. If Coetzee deals with the South African situation in *Waiting for the Barbarians*, it is through the allegory that characterizes this narrative and allows for his implicit critique of Empire to travel to other colonial locations. In 1981, Gordimer wrote *July's People*, a novel that depicts the quintessential interregnum moment she describes in her 1982 essay "Living in the Interregnum," as the white protagonist Maureen Smales runs toward an unknown future during a fictional South African civil uprising—the same fictive uprising, perhaps, that Coetzee later explores in *Age of Iron*, a novel he published in 1990, the same year Nelson Mandela was freed from prison.

Since the end of apartheid in 1994, South African authors have had to come to terms with the construct known as the "new" South Africa, a place where the vestiges of a history of racial oppression still occupy the major part of the narrative frame. Many South African authors struggle, as playwright Malcolm Purkey claims that he is doing, to find a "new fiction" and a "new enemy"—an external nemesis—against which to pit their work.[3] Similarly, literary critics are seeking new ways of identifying, classifying, and categorizing South African literature as it exists and continues to emerge from a legacy of colonial imposition. In his study, *A History of South African Literature*, for example, Christopher Heywood attempts to "overfly the colonial past" by approaching the categories of "English, Afrikaans, Coloured, and Black . . . as a single subject" (vii). And while Nadine Gordimer's recent novel *The Pickup* (2001) is set initially in South Africa, the protagonist Julie Summers emigrates with her lover Abdu to his unnamed Arab village. In a literary move uncharacteristic of her writing career, Gordimer's narrative is set, at least in part, in an unspecified location—a location beyond the boundaries of post-apartheid South Africa. It seems rather ironic, then, that at this tumultuous and shifting literary moment, Coetzee's second Booker Prize winning novel *Disgrace* (1999) emerged as arguably his most realistic and political novel, set firmly within the post-apartheid present of South Africa. At the end of the twentieth century, it seemed that perhaps Gordimer and Coetzee had engaged in a paradigm shift that may have—once again—displaced critical ability to characterize Coetzee as Gordimer's "other."

Nadine Gordimer and J. M. Coetzee, as South Africa's two predominant contemporary white writers of fiction, are often cast in relief against one another as authors with vastly different approaches to their artistic treatment of the political situation in South Africa, a situation that artists, many critics claim, have an ethical responsibility to realistically represent. And the South African artist's primary responsibility has been to represent the race-based injustices inherent in South Africa's history, injustices that have—perhaps with good reason—outweighed other potential political and ethical concerns. For example, while Gordimer is undeniably and admittedly political in her work, writing explicitly against apartheid, her writing is less concerned with feminist issues. As Stephen Clingman notes in *The Essential Gesture,* "women's liberation in South Africa, as far as [Gordimer] was concerned, was attendant upon and secondary to more fundamental economic and political change" (199). Coetzee's writing, by contrast, is always evasive of an overt political stance, confessional, anti-apartheid, feminist, or otherwise. Such nonparticipation has led to charges of complicity and anti-feminism, or to the somewhat reductive claim that, because he often refuses to locate his narratives in any "real" location, Coetzee writes "parables of, among other things, the contemporary political situation in the Republic of South Africa" (Merivale 153). Critical defense of Coetzee's evasive position, on the other hand, is most often characterized by claims like Jane Poyner's that Coetzee's tendency to write against confession and realistic representational narrative as well as a supposed tendency not to voice black South African characters "constitutes a scrupulously defined political position: as (unwilling) representative of the colonial oppressor, Coetzee refuses to assert the (hi)stories of the Other, to impose meaning on them" (67).

Whether read through a positive or negative lens, however, Coetzee's political silences, especially in the context of South Africa, must be recognized as conscious acts of resistance against the kind of realistic representation that is expected and in many ways required of South African artists. Yet Coetzee's writing is implicitly political by virtue of its resistance, a resistance engendered by many of his characters. Acts of resistance are in themselves political as they constitute reactions to (or more specifically, against) a political situation or the agreed-upon expression of a political situation. Furthermore, such resistance, in as much as it marks a refusal to accept political and historical narratives as de facto truths, is an ethical analysis of representation: by refusing to present the decided-upon version of political events, Coetzee's narratives engage with the ethics of accepting *any* representation as the truth. Therefore, I have argued previously that Coetzee's work functions as minor literature[4] by highlighting the ways that "each individual intrigue" is connected to the larger framework of politics (Deleuze and Guattari 17).[5] But whether or not Coetzee's narrative strategies destabilize claims that his writing either usurps a voice that is not his own (as far as his female narrators are concerned) or fails to realistically represent, or voice, black South Africans, the continual debate about the ethical responsibility of the artist is situated within the theoretical interregnum that characterizes the transitional natures of South African society and literature.

The presence of a theoretical interregnum has become a defining aspect of South African literature and history as a result of Nadine Gordimer's aforementioned essay, "Living in the Interregnum." Despite the literal meaning of "interregnum" as the interval between the end of one sovereign's reign and the accession of the next legitimate successor, philosopher Antonio Gramsci redefined the term when he interpreted it within the context of Marxist revolution. The interregnum, according to Gramsci, is the temporal period during which "the old is dying, and the new cannot be born; in this interregnum there arises a great diversity of morbid symptoms."[6] This interregnum, claims Gramsci, results from a crisis of authority: "if the ruling class has lost its consensus; i.e. is no longer 'leading' but only 'dominant,' exercising coercive force alone, this means precisely that the masses have become detached from their traditional ideologies" during which time, in conjunction with "morbid symptoms," there also arises "the possibility and necessity of creating a new culture" (276). Therefore, the "legitimate" ruler—the ruler dictated by birthright or consensus—that characterizes a more traditional understanding of the interregnum, is, in Gramsci's sense, absent from the Marxist conception of the interregnum as a transitional period of tumultuous, revolutionary uncertainty situated within a capitalist framework.

Frantz Fanon's explanation of decolonization seemingly takes Gramsci's Marxist dictum and interprets it within a colonial context where the Marxist categories of laborer and ruling class are less applicable, a context in which a capitalist system is imposed upon an indigenous population by external colonial forces: while Gramsci's interregnum creates the necessity for a new culture after a transitional period of uncertainty, for Fanon, "decolonization is quite simply the replacing of one 'species' of men by another 'species' of men. *Without any period of transition,* there is a total, complete, and absolute substitution" (35, my emphasis). Given its complex colonial history involving not only Dutch colonization in 1652 of the indigenous Khoikhoi and San (often erroneously conflated as "Khoisan") peoples—their own kingdoms fractured through internal warfare as early as the third century A.D.—British colonization in 1805, and apartheid from 1948 to 1994, South African history can be read through both Marxist and postcolonial lenses.

According to Francisco Ascui,

> Gramsci's 'interregnum' . . . is neither static nor specific to any particular period. . . . It describes a process of transition that takes place in every age, rather than an event: there is always an old world dying, and new worlds are ever struggling to be born. ("Multiculturalism")

As such, the term "interregnum" has become a floating signifier[7] of sorts, capable of traveling from context to context in ways that the more historically and event-specific term "decolonization" cannot, at least in its current usage. In "Living in the Interregnum," Gordimer applies Gramsci's interpretation of this intermediate period to the social and political uncertainty that characterized South Africa during the state of continuous civil unrest of the 1970s and early 1980s. According to Stephen Clingman, Gordimer's application of Gramsci's concept of the interregnum to this period of South African history provides her essay with two particular strengths: "one is the full realisation that South Africa was already in a state of revolution, and had been so for some time. The second is the awareness that this was not an unambiguous condition" (*Essential* 261). Gordimer describes her position "at 6,000 feet in a society whirling, stamping, swaying with the force of revolutionary change," heading toward an unknown future that will be characterized by "the black state that is coming" (264). The Gramscian interregnum, as a result of Gordimer's explication of the term as a state of "Hegel's disintegrated consciousness, of contradictions" that is "not only between two social orders but also between two identities, one known and discarded, the other unknown and undetermined" (269–70), has become a defining aspect of

much South African literature that is characterized by a focus on the immediate, by the notion of "now," in the wake of an uncertain and sometimes
apocalyptic vision[8] of the future.

While it would be overstatement to claim that all of South African literature is characterized by its attention to the interregnum, the space
between the end of apartheid (or in fiction written before the implementa-
tion of apartheid, the end of some facet of colonial domination) and the
beginning of a new political paradigm has certainly been the historical
moment—even an unforeseeable fictive future moment depicted in literature
written prior to the end of apartheid—upon which much South African literature has focused. Even after apartheid ended, the "new" South Africa has
in many ways found itself in another interregnum, according to Thomas
Ohlson and Stephen John Stedman, a "second interregnum" that "differs
from that of the 1980s in two important respects. People's expectations
about and demands for change have grown, and profound uncertainty about
what form that change would take has raised the political stakes for all concerned" (2). The space between the end of apartheid and a new South
African political order has extended into the present, and no social or gov-
ernmental movement has enabled South Africa to envision a future divorced
from the legacy of its past. Despite the fact that it is possible to be hopeful
about South Africa's future, to believe, as Robert I. Rotberg does, that "there
is a palpable sense of renewal, and quiet optimism," that optimism is never
far removed from the reality of "brutal, continuing internal wars, . . . the persistence of poverty, and the alarming devastation caused by AIDS and other
diseases" (499). South Africans are still waiting for the means to achieve sus-
tainable and equitable economic growth well over a decade after the immediate collapse of apartheid's codification of racial oppression and legacy of civil
unrest, and in her essay, Gordimer claims that neither Marxist communism
nor Western capitalism can provide a viable solution to the emergent "new"
South Africa's formative problems.

By contrast, I contend that the interregnum "now" of J. M. Coetzee's fiction is never temporal, and with very few exceptions, never tied concretely to a
specific historical time and place. Even when Coetzee's texts do portray some
identifiable historical moment, like the contemporary South Africa of *Disgrace,*
Coetzee's interregnum is conceptual, illustrative of the idea that any time two
or more people can conceive of the merest possibility of disrupting the binaries
that define their relationships and thereby engage reciprocally with one
another, the secular limbo of the interregnum may (possibly, potentially, but
certainly not probably) give way to the unknown and unknowable future.
Whereas Gordimer claims in "Living in the Interregnum" that "nothing I say

here will be as true as my fiction" (264), Coetzee's literary interregnum is defined through various forms of narrative displacement, conscious refusals by both author and characters to ascribe any status to consistent notions of "the truth," either in fiction or in more ostensibly objective modes of historical discourse. Coetzee's interregnum is the space between inaction and the ability to recognize the possibility for action, the moment after a dialogic question is asked but before an answer can be formulated—a seemingly minute distance that is nonetheless characterized by an immense and nearly impossible cognitive leap. This interregnum is an illusive space outside of not only history, but outside of all binary relationships, the space established by Coetzee's character of Michael K, who discovers "that it is enough to be . . . out of all the camps at the same time" (182), despite everyone else's best efforts to categorize and define his subject position.

As a result of Coetzee's resistance to categorization and to representing recognizable places and realistic historical occurrences, Coetzee's primary major critics, Teresa Dovey, Dominic Head, and David Attwell, ascribe allegorical status to much of his work. While criticism about Coetzee's work has historically tended to focus on three overarching issues—resistance to confessional narrative, allegory, and Coetzee's engagement with and reworking of Hegel's master/slave dialectic—with the most discussed of these, as Dominic Head states, being "the question of historical engagement, and the appropriate fictional response to the apartheid regime" (8), the arguments for allegory in Coetzee's writing influence the other two. The use of allegory in postcolonial literature in general, as coded writing, has long been debated,[9] and the concept of the allegorical has been applied to Coetzee's writing in particular as "a network of deferments of meaning, of allusions to (and substitutions for) an unattainable referent" (Head 21). Furthermore, according to Dovey, allegory

> provides a temporary resting place for the repetitive dialectical movement of irony. In Coetzee's novels, this resting place may be located between their allegorical readings of the texts of the tradition, and the allegorical writing of their own evocation of the response of the Other in a future of potential readings. (43)

For Dovey, Coetzee's allegorical writing provides a critique of various modes of writing as "master narratives," a claim that may prove somewhat contentious given Coetzee's recent acceptance of the Nobel Prize, a distinction that in many ways defines him as the creator of a particular *type* of master narrative.

In his new study, *J. M. Coetzee and the Ethics of Reading,* Derek Attridge takes up the issue of allegory and claims that "we need to ask how allegory is thematized in the fiction, and whether this staging of allegory as an *issue* provides any guidance in talking about Coetzee's *use* of allegory" (34). Such a reading gives credence to the performative, the metafictional, and the self-conscious act of writing that Coetzee undertakes in all of his work, and ascribes to the author a conscious agency in the "use" of allegory as a tool to, essentially, allegorize the allegorical. Furthermore, Dovey claims that the metafictional analysis inherent in Coetzee's work disrupts the master/slave dialectic through the allegorical mode of his writing by exposing the myth of a master narrative. While Dovey, Head, and Attwell examine Coetzee's refusal to engage with various entities—history, South African politics, realistic writing—and the ways that his characters actively refuse to engage in reciprocal relationships (Michael K) or are thwarted and misguided in their attempts at reciprocity (Magda, the Magistrate), this book examines the places where connection—or the idea of connection—may be, if not possible in itself, at least possible to imagine, and explores, instead of allegory, the performative fables that fill the specific interregnum space that Coetzee's work occupies.

In this study, I read Coetzee's narratives as performative examinations of the nature of imagined identification with the other, in the form of not only the black characters who are often silent in his texts (Friday in *Foe* and the trio of rapists in *Disgrace,* for example) and white women who often narrate, but also in the form of animals, especially the dogs that populate almost all of Coetzee's opus. These various entities represent multiple subjectivities, none of which belongs to the author who must imagine them. In order to represent this diversity of others, therefore, Coetzee's narrative strategies— free indirect discourse in many of his third-person narrated texts that feature male protagonists (*Life & Times of Michael K, The Master of Petersburg,* and *Disgrace*), various and differing first-person narrative accounts of the same story (*Dusklands, In the Heart of the Country*), the use of female narrators and female narrative personas (*Age of Iron, The Lives of Animals*), and unlocatable, ahistorical contexts (*Waiting for the Barbarians*)—destabilize expectations and alienate the reader from the willing suspension of disbelief that generally accompanies readings of fiction. Such destabilization opens up a space for the audience to examine the constructed nature of Coetzee's fiction as texts that allow for interplay between character, audience, and author; the text performs various positions rather than presents one controlling subjectivity, and the audience is alternately invited to participate in the performance. Read as performative, Coetzee's texts create the potential for imagined identification with the various others that populate them, and reading Coetzee's narratives as performative allows for a degree of transparency: one can, after all, perform the other's voice or silence—and we accept that the performance will always be mimetic, an approximation of the "real" thing rather than a usurpation of the voice of the other. Furthermore, I read such performances—acknowledged by Coetzee himself within his metafictional narratives—as evidence of the limits of the sympathetic imagination. These performances ask of both characters and audience, if we are unable to imagine the interiority of an alternate subjectivity, whether that subjectivity belongs to a member of another race, sex, or species, what is our responsibility to that other? Coetzee's narratives illustrate the ethical responsibility that must be undertaken on a personal level in the absence of reciprocity, whether real or imaginary.

* * *

Coetzee's narratives are performative by virtue of the fact that Coetzee displaces not only the narrative voice—through his use of female narrators, Magda in *In the Heart of the Country* (1982), Susan Barton in *Foe* (1986), and Elizabeth Curren in *Age of Iron* (1990)—but also the authoritative voice—through his embodiment of the female subject position in the lectures he attributes to the persona of Elizabeth Costello in "The Novel in Africa" (1999), *The Lives of Animals* (1999), "Elizabeth Costello and the Problem of Evil" (2003) and the other "Costello Lectures" that constitute the novel *Elizabeth Costello* (2003). Via these narrative displacements, Coetzee imagines and performs a subject position other than his own, that of a white woman. Displacement, claims Trinh T. Minh-Ha, is a mode of resistance in that it "involves the invention of new forms of subjectivities . . . of relationships, which also implies the continuous renewal of values to which one refers in fabricating the tools of resistance" (217). The various displacements that Coetzee practices serve to present the interaction of multiple subjectivities as performed dialogue without putting the author in the position of speaking "for" the other. Such a stance allows his narratives to shed light on subject positions that neither author nor audience may occupy.

Coetzee, therefore, writes dialogically in the Bahktinian sense, as one who refuses to claim the narrative position of the monologic insider, the textual presence that has access to the answers, or access to contested notions of the truth. According to Bahktin,

> the word in living conversation is directly, blatantly, oriented toward a
> future answer-word: it provokes an answer, anticipates it and structures

itself in the answer's direction. Forming itself in an atmosphere of the
already spoken, the word is at the same time determined by that which
has not yet been said but which is needed and in fact anticipated by the
answering word. Such is the situation in any living dialogue. (280)

The notion of "that which has not yet been said" has particularly strong reso-
nances in terms of the conceptual interregnum in which my work places
Coetzee's writing. While Gramsci's notion of the interregnum clearly foresees
a specific revolutionary paradigm that will, at some unspecified point,
replace that which is dying, Bahktin's dialogism indicates that that which has
not yet been said is unknown and unknowable. Therefore, the potential for
the unforeseeable to become manifest is always alluded to in terms of the
dialogic. As I have said before, it is the potential for—not the manifestation
of—action or enunciation that characterizes Coetzee's fiction.

   In discussing Dostoevsky's status as a practitioner of the dialogic
novel, Coetzee makes a case for the importance of the performative in terms
of dialogism:

> writing dialogically means writing in a manner which respects the
> knowledge of all who participate in the fiction. It's a notion that comes
> quite naturally to drama but doesn't come so naturally to long works of
> fiction, because in drama there is a natural dialogue between the charac-
> ters. In fiction . . . there tends to be some controlling position, either
> latent or patent, someone who knows what's going on in a way that the
> characters don't. (Wachtel 44)[10]

While Coetzee does not write drama, his writing does refuse a controlling
narrative position and raises dialogic questions about embodiment as a kind
of performance—acting as the other—that is potentially possible through
imagined identification with the bodily suffering of the other. According to
Coetzee, "in South Africa it is not possible to deny the authority of suffering
and therefore the body" because "it is not that one *grants* the authority of the
suffering body: the suffering body *takes* this authority: that is its power"
(*Doubling* 248). The truth, if there is any such thing as the truth, can only be
obtained through the equalizing and paralinguistic suffering of the body, the
body with which those who do not suffer can identify only through imagination or through the imitative performance of an alternate subject position.
The bodies with which Coetzee's characters and audience are asked to engage
in imagined physical dialogue not only consist of white women and racially
designated others, but also of animals.

Such imagined dialogue is difficult given that the subject position of both Coetzee and his protagonists—male, female, and animal—is characterized by a refusal to confess "the truth," because for Coetzee, confession always raises "problems regarding truthfulness, problems whose common factor seems to be a regression to infinity of self-awareness and self-doubt" ("Confession" 274). In *Life & Times of Michael K* (1983), for example, Michael refuses to "confess" his story to anyone who asks just as in *The Master of Petersburg* (1994), despite his claim that "I'm not asking you to confess" (195), Dostoevsky seeks the reasons for his stepson's death from the police, from Nechaev, and from a dog tied out in the cold, only to be met with refusal from all three. Because they refuse to engage with history through acts of confession, Coetzee's narratives are situated outside of traditional understandings of not only postcolonial and postmodern writing but are also located outside of any consistent notion of historical or personal truth. Coetzee refuses to offer insight into the realm of the outside, claiming that he will not "produce a master narrative for a set of texts that claim to deny all master narratives" (Morphet 464). Such a task would be impossible given Coetzee's admission that "the heart of our own desire is unknown to us" (Wachtel 45): there is no interpretation that Coetzee can offer because all interpretation is suspect, the product of potentially self-indulgent and confessional analysis.

Coetzee's writing, through such acts of refusal that constitute a specific mode of performative displacement, also enacts narrative *Verfremdungseffekts* or alienation effects characteristic of Brechtian theater. Brecht claims that "a representation that alienates . . . allows us to recognize its subject, but at the same time makes it seem unfamiliar. The classical and medieval theatre alienated its characters by making them wear human or animal masks" (192). Furthermore, Elin Diamond claims that in Brecht's epic theater,

> the actor "alienates" rather than impersonates her character, she "quotes" or demonstrates the character's behavior instead of identifying with it. Brecht theorizes that if the performer remains *outside* the character's feelings, the audience may also and thus freely analyze and form opinions about the play's "fable." (Diamond 45, my emphasis)

In "The Narrative of Jacobus Coetzee," the second of the two novellas that comprise *Dusklands,* there are various tellings and retellings of an authentic historical document that appears in the appendix, a deposition made by Jacobus Coetzee in 1760. The various documents that make up Jacobus's narrative are presented as historical truths, but, as Sheila Collingwood-Whittick claims, "within the body of the text the 'real' author plants clues and markers whose clear objective is precisely to expose the 'fiction' of histori- cal veracity" ("J. M. Coetzee's" 76). These markers constitute alienation effects that destabilize the reader's perception of narrative truth and allow the reader access to the "moral" of the work, the instability of historical narrative.

The use of the term "fable" in Diamond's description of the alienation effect is indicative of a potential moral message highlighted as a result of such effects. In terms of my reading of Coetzee's writing, however, "fable" takes on its more originary meaning as a tale that employs animal characters in order to teach a moral, and such a reading also speaks to Brecht's example of the animal masks worn in classical and medieval drama: in "The Narrative of Jacobus Coetzee," Jacobus essentially "masks" the native South African peo- ples by referring to them as animals—"the Bushman is a . . . wild animal with an animal's soul" (58)—in order to distance or alienate himself from any identification with these people. Coetzee's subsequent novels decon- struct such maskings by refusing to treat animals either metaphorically or anthropomorphically and instead present animals as animals, devoid of a fic- tionally representable interiority. Therefore, the animal body presents the greatest challenge to imagined identification with an alternate subjectivity, and the animals that populate many of Coetzee's texts—including *The Mas- ter of Petersburg* and *Disgrace* among others—are animals whose bodies are disruptively positioned within the narratives between various binary con- structions that determine master/slave relationships. Coetzee's fables cannot, therefore, be allegorical; in Coetzee's fiction, the animal body does not find one-to-one correlation with some unrepresentable abstraction. Instead, the animal body is a body, voiceless and suffering, engaged within in a social and historical milieu—the interregnum—characterized by its status as similarly inarticulate.

Coetzee's presentation of the animal as an animal disrupts what I have termed the primary binary opposition of animal/human that is dependent upon a monolithic narrative position and that underscores all forms of sub- sequent othering. In Coetzee's fables of imagined identification, the animal as trope moves from the wild creatures that populate the pre-colonial South African landscape, to a specific domesticated (or colonized) creature, the dog. Similarly, over the course of South African colonial and literary history, within certain indigenous and colonial contexts, the animal shifts from a source of sustenance—as cattle, for example—to a metaphor for the sub- human qualities attributed to the indigenous South African peoples by their various colonial conquerors. Coetzee's work charts this progression, from simile in *Dusklands* (1974) to symbol in *The Master of Petersburg.* In *Dis- grace,* the animal body is rendered literal and liberated from its status as a symbolic and linguistic phenomenon: the dog becomes a dog within an historical tradition that has always represented various groups of people *as* dogs. In Coetzee's fiction, the recognition of the alterity of animals marks an initial step—or, rather, a potential initial step—in the displacement of the binary constructions of colonizer and colonized, man and woman, culture and nature, and, most importantly, self and other.

Human oppression of the animal may provide a basis for the oppression of humans by humans; alternately, reciprocity between humans and animals may provide the basis for the breakdown of such oppression. To view animals as deserving of the respect and love granted to them by Lucy Lurie and Bev Shaw in *Disgrace* and voiced by Coetzee as he performs the female persona of Elizabeth Costello in *The Lives of Animals* is to begin to undo the Western binary philosophical thinking that Judith Butler claims "depends on the exclusion of women, slaves, children, and animals" and that operates "through the production of racialized Others" (*Bodies* 48). Coetzee productively restores various incarnations of what feminist-vegetarian theorist Carol J. Adams refers to as the absent referent[11]—woman, animal, child, black South African—not only through vegetarian characters such as Lucy and through Coetzee's performance of Costello, but also by allowing animals to mediate the space between dualities *as* animals, not as symbolic representations of other oppressed groups of humans.[12]

* * *

Chapter Two of this study details literary and social history in South Africa with regard to animals as this history has influenced Coetzee's subsequent representations of animals in his fiction from *Dusklands* to *Disgrace*. Wild and domestic animals have played a large part in South Africa's colonial and apartheid history, and this chapter examines the role of animals in South Africa from the time of the Khoikhoi and San people in the fifteenth century to the Xhosa cattle killing of 1856–57, during which the Xhosa slaughtered over 400,000 cattle in response to prophecies indicating that such action would drive white settlers away from South Africa. Furthermore, in this chapter I discuss the implications of current environmental animal-related crises in South Africa and analyze characterizations of animals in South African literature from Olive Schreiner's *Story of an African Farm* (1883) to Zakes Mda's *Heart of Redness* (2002). Other texts that I examine include Sarah Gertrude Millin's *God's Stepchildren* (1924), Sol Plaatje's *Mhudi* (1930), Alan Paton's *Cry the Beloved Country* (1948), Bloke Modisane's *Blame Me on History* (1963), Nadine Gordimer's *Burger's Daughter* (1979), and Sindiwe Magona's *Mother to Mother* (1998). These novels provide a comparative basis for examining Coetzee's work as it charts the progression from the literary trope of animals as wild creatures to domesticated companions, from simile in his first work of fiction, the two novellas that constitute *Dusklands,* to symbol in the more recent *The Master of Petersburg.* In this chapter, I focus predominantly on these two novels, but I also trace the various dogs that move through all of Coetzee's works. In his fiction, Coetzee makes clear the connection between the destruction of animals and the othering of human beings, including women and indigenous Africans, an othering that theoretically began with the historical shift from nomadic, hunter/gatherer societies to agriculturally based societies indicative of the beginnings of "culture."

In Chapter Three, I focus on Coetzee's displacement of the colonizing voice through the creation of his female narrators of Magda in *In the Heart of the Country* (1977), Susan Barton in *Foe* (1986), and Elizabeth Curren in *Age of Iron* (1990). Just as I argue that the dog shifts from simile to symbol to signified in Coetzee's corpus, the position of his female narrators shifts from linguistic entity (Magda exists in large part only as a metaphoric critique of narrative construction) to metafictional interloper (Susan Barton attempts to control Daniel Foe's narrative of Robinson Cruso) to Coetzeean persona (Elizabeth Curren occupies the same socio-economic, racial, and employment strata as her creator). Coetzee's female narrators also operate via a kind of Brechtian alienation effect to decenter and remove authority from the narrative position as the female voice becomes an exercise in the possible failure of writerly performance: Magda writes and rewrites her story, alternately creating and then negating her very existence; Susan Barton wants to write her story of a shipwrecked existence but is unable to write anything other than Foe's narrative; and Elizabeth Curren writes a letter—a letter that may never be delivered—in which she attempts to explain her life and her illness to her daughter in the United States. I read Susan Barton and Elizabeth Curren as potential future incarnations of Magda, as characters that enrich our understandings of several concepts introduced in *In the Heart of the Country:* how one—especially a woman—writes oneself into history, and the difficulty of occupying a definitive position during a colonial, apartheid, and/or gendered interregnum.

Chapter Four focuses on the characters of the Magistrate in *Waiting for the Barbarians* (1980) and Michael in *Life & Times of Michael K* and the consequences of their resistance to signification within an oppressive system that demands the binary thinking inherent in the mechanization of war. Even when Coetzee's narration does occupy the first-person male subject position, as it does *in Waiting for the Barbarians,* or when his protagonist is male, as is the case in the third-person narrated *Life & Times of Michael K,* his writing is nonetheless marked by a refusal to embody a position and voice complicit with the colonial impulse; even the first-person male narrated components of *Dusklands,* while ostensibly maintaining a pro-colonial voice, undermine such a stance by providing a metanarrative critique of not only the truth of such "historical" narratives, but also of the "benefits" of the history that such narratives seek to impart. In these texts, acts of refusal, whether through silence (as are Michael's) or through action (as are the Magistrate's), further displace the narrative voice and position the male perspective outside of the privileged, imperialist subjectivity Coetzee initially critiques in *Dusklands.* In *Life & Times of Michael K,* Michael's refusal to confess, to tell his story to anyone, whether friend or foe, is comparable to the Magistrate's refusal to disclose the details of his journey to return a supposed "barbarian" girl to her people, a silence foreshadowed by the girl's refusal to disclose the details of her torture to the Magistrate. But whereas the Magistrate admits to being on a road to nowhere at the end of the *Waiting for the Barbarians,* Michael's persistent existence at the end of *Life & Times of Michael K* maintains the potential for an altered future. Both characters, however, are unable to experience an existence outside of that determined by their historical contexts; if there is any access to the outside in these narratives, it is only available in the characters' ability, however limited, to imagine an alternate reality.

Chapter Five is characterized by a quote from Jacqueline Rose's article on the Truth and Reconciliation Commission in which she references J. M. Coetzee's *The Lives of Animals.* She says "intellectuals are always accused of talking too much, not acting enough"(178). This chapter focuses on the disjunction between intellectualism and activism and between the spoken and the enacted in *The Lives of Animals* and *Disgrace.* It brings together all of the threads—narrative displacement and alienation effect, performance of an alternate subjectivity and the reinterpretation of traditional notions of fable—that I discuss in the earlier chapters of this work. The action that takes place in *The Lives of Animals* in particular is performative, Coetzee's fully realized mimetic exercise in embodiment, the manifestation of an implicit critique of all forms of imagined identification—with fictional characters, with animals, and with women. In *The Lives of Animals,* Coetzee addresses the ethics of meat-eating and animal experimentation via the persona of Elizabeth Costello, a character who claims that she can imagine the consciousness of an animal: "I can think my way into the existence of a bat or a chimpanzee or an oyster" (35). In *The Lives of Animals,* therefore, Coetzee performs Costello who *acts* by virtue of her vegetarian ethics.

In *Disgrace,* however, Coetzee's narrative refuses to offer analogous relationships between the treatment of animals and the treatment of humans, and it is in *Disgrace* that the failure of the sympathetic imagination is most fully apparent. *Disgrace* illustrates the possibility of secular redemption even as protagonist David Lurie attempts, unsuccessfully, to imagine the rape of his daughter Lucy from Lucy's perspective. It would be easy to fall back on anthropomorphism in this narrative, to use the dogs that populate the text as symbols for Lucy, but the dog that David Lurie "sacrifices" at the end of the narrative is a dog, not a symbolic representation of Lucy or of any of the other characters. In *Disgrace* the dog is not a simile used to represent the black South Africans who live on the farm with Lucy (nor the three black men who rape her), nor is the dog a pet to be pampered by white South Africans while township children starve. David's resignation to his inability to imagine Lucy's experience is perhaps a kernel of his recognition of the alterity of the other. Because he cannot imagine the interiority of either his daughter, his student Melanie with whom he has an illicit sexual relationship, the dogs whose bodies he delivers to the dump, or the black South Africans who have lived under the rule of apartheid, David may ultimately learn to respect the alterity of that which he cannot successfully perform or embody. David's potential acceptance of his alienation from the various others with whom he seeks to identify is what allows the reader to maintain hope in the face of this, Coetzee's most bleak presentation of the "new" South Africa.

Chapter Two
Coetzee's Dogs from Simile to Signified: South African History, Environment, and Literature

The cattle are the people. The people are the cattle. (John Edgar Wideman, *The Cattle Killing* 7)

The conclusion I have reached is that, above all, dogs are witnesses. They are allowed access to our most private moments. They are there when we think we are alone. . . . If they could tell us everything they have seen, all the gaps of our lives would stitch themselves together. (Carolyn Parkhurst, *The Dogs of Babel* 14)

As I have previously stated, in Coetzee's works, animals move from the wild creatures—giraffes, elephants, and hares—that populate the pre-colonial South African landscape, to a very specific domesticated and therefore "colonized" animal, the dog. Similarly, over the course of South African colonial and literary history, within certain indigenous and colonial contexts, the animal has shifted from livestock, a source of subsistence, to metaphor for the sub-human qualities attributed to the indigenous South African peoples by white colonial forces. Coetzee's work charts this progression, from simile in *Dusklands* (1974) to both symbol and signified entity in *The Master of Petersburg* (1994). In this chapter, after a preliminary examination of animals in a larger body of South African fiction, I will focus predominantly on two enabling animal-centered fables that shape the choices of the protagonists in these two specific works, but I will also trace the trope of the dog as it moves through all of Coetzee's fiction to date. In "The Narrative of Jacobus Coetzee," the second component of *Dusklands*, Jacobus's belief that his ability to kill animals is what distinguishes him from them is the enabling narrative that he tells himself in order to justify his perceived difference from the native South Africans that he treats *like* animals. In *The Master of Petersburg*, Dostoevsky's belief that the dog tied out in the cold is not the sign that he is seeking enables him to continue to search for esoteric signs instead of reacting to the explicit suffering taking place directly in front of him.

The exploitation of animals in South Africa's colonial and apartheid history has never been far removed from the degradation of the environment and the oppression of indigenous South African peoples by colonial forces, and this legacy continues up to the present day. In the early twentieth century, for example, South African environmental problems were mainly the result of overgrazing of livestock (Beinart and Coates 63), and in the latter half, "deforestation and soil erosion have followed in the wake of the movement of refugees and displaced persons" (Ohlson and Stedman 297-8). While precolonial Africans did slaughter animals, hunting was for subsistence and sacrificial purposes only. However, indigenous hunting practices became enmeshed with those of white hunters during the 1800s when ivory was the chief export of the Transvaal (Beinart and Coates 21), and despite the fact that the demand for ivory decreased during the latter part of the nineteenth century—replaced by consumer desire for another product derived from animal exploitation, silk—the elephant continues to exist in a state of dangerous decline in large part because of the contribution of its ivory to the financial cost of civil unrest in the region. According to Thomas Ohlson and Stephen John Stedman, for example, "one hundred thousand elephants were slaughtered in Angola in the 1980s . . . to pay South Africa for its support" (297) during a period of war. The conservationist mentality has contributed to national parks and wildlife protection areas that have benefited some endangered species, but such strategies operate in part by providing an attractive option "for white environmental concern because they furnish a route out of the central conservationist mentality: how to enjoy the advantage of urban-industrial society while salvaging a modicum of nature" (Beinart and Coates 93). That modicum is relegated to an area behind a fence, a place that provides the illusion, according to Joy Williams, that "you have entered a portion of the earth that wild animals have retained possession of. The illusion here is that wild animals exist" ("Safariland" 27). Animals die against the fence, trapped as they seek to migrate and extend their man-made boundaries into a depleted environment where they are no longer welcome.

The animal as a literal entity has always been present within the South African landscape, as a means of precolonial subsistence and conversely in colonial literature about the Dutch East India Company's garden at the Cape of Good Hope (Coetzee, *White Writing* 1). Furthermore, the animal in South Africa has also functioned as a locus for colonial displacement, acting as an historical and literary scapegoat, a site of putative retribution for the projected fears of colonizer and colonized alike. The most familiar reference to the scapegoat is recorded in the Bible, in Leviticus 16:20 -22:

> [Aaron] is to lay both of his hands on the goat's head and confess over it all the sins and rebellion of the Israelites. In this way, he will lay the people's sins on the head of the goat; then he will send it out into the wilderness, led by a man chosen for this task. After the man sets it free in the wilderness, the goat will carry all the people's sins upon itself into a desolate land.

While the concept of the scapegoat is perhaps best known in its biblical incarnation, the scapegoat mentality, the displacement of responsibility and/or blame onto the body of the animal, functions as an archetypal trope. The scapegoat myth underlies the historical narrative of the Xhosa cattle killing in South Africa, an event that has had a profound effect on both subsequent literature and life in South Africa and abroad.[1] But the historical and symbolic role of cattle in South African culture is not limited to the Xhosa cattle killing; it is omnipresent, from the time that the Khoikhoi people broke with the hunter San, for whom "control over hunting for the distribution of meat, and particularly trade in ivory, were mechanisms for asserting power, stamping territorial authority, and defining gender roles" (Beinart and Coates 19). Sometime before the fifteenth century, the Khoikhoi began to cultivate livestock, and in the communal culture of the Khoikhoi people, "livestock was by far the most valued form of private property in a society where land was never divided among individuals" (Elphick 59). Despite the value placed on livestock, according to Richard Elphick, "neither sheep nor cattle were regularly slaughtered. Slaughter was undertaken chiefly to celebrate special occasions . . . or as a sacrifice to combat illness among humans or stock" (60); milk was a much more valued nutritional source because it did not require depletion of an owner's livestock population. Furthermore, the fact that animal sacrifice was practiced to save livestock as well as humans clearly indicates the value placed upon livestock animals by the Khoikhoi, a value that, while it may have been predicated on the need for the subsistence that animals allotted, is at least structured upon a sense of respect for the inherent value of the animal.

By the late 1600s, however, the Khoikhoi lost their livestock in large part because of the Dutch East India Company's policies of robbery and military action as well as by virtue of the Dutch colonizers' "spread of new diseases, interdiction of chiefly aggrandizement, expropriation of pastures, [and] demand for Khoikhoi labor" (Elphick 174). As the Cape settlers moved inland, they appropriated not only large tracts of land, but also any livestock that was on that land (Ohlson and Stedman 21). The contested role of cattle in South Africa was still apparent well into the twentieth century, when "voluntary" removals, like the Mogopa removal of 1984, for example, forced black South Africans to leave their farms and sell their cattle for mere pittance to Boer farmers. Because "cattle are a measure of a man's success in the villages" (Goodman 325), the loss of cattle that one had cared for and seen increase over generations was not only a devastating financial blow, but was also akin to the loss of a kind of ancestral memory, the loss of a history dependent upon human and animal co-dependency and interaction.

For a people like the Xhosa, that ancestral memory is tainted by such a loss, but a loss of much more devastating proportions. During the cattle killing, the cattle became the scapegoat of the Xhosa people who felt that butchering their animals and destroying their crops would guarantee the disappearance of the white settlers from South Africa. A young girl named Nongqawuse prophesied the end of colonial rule and a return to a precolonial utopia, "as they had been Embo, in the very beginning" (Magona 180), if the Xhosa slaughtered all of their animals. According to J. B. Peires in his seminal work on the cattle killing, *The Dead Will Arise*, Nongqawuse claimed that

> On the great day, two suns would rise red in the sky over the mountain of Ntaba kaNdoda where they would collide and darkness would cover the earth. . . . Then the righteous dead . . . and the new cattle would rise . . . . The English . . . would retreat into the sea, which would rise up in two walls to engulf them and open a road for them. (98)

After over 400,000 cattle were slaughtered and the prophecies unfulfilled, mass starvation resulted causing the Xhosa population to drop from 105,000 in January of 1857 to 25,916 a year later (Peires 319). Subsequently, over 600,000 acres of Xhosa land was lost to whites. It is little wonder that the killing as an historical marker finds its way into much South African literature.[2]

It would seem that in order to begin to undo the environmental and human tolls of the capitalist colonial enterprise, a preemptive—or perhaps disruptive—strategy is needed, one that attempts neither to return South

Africa to a mythic precolonial ideal nor to act solely at the end of South African history. One such strategy involves an examination of the relationship between animals and humans within the colonial, capitalist model. In such a system, the animal body is commodified, rendered an item of exchange, because, according to Beinart and Coates, "a central aspect of modern consumer society . . . is the consumption of nature as a part of the good life. It grows out of the territorial aggrandizement of the paraphernalia of modernity" (98). Such thinking is a foundational aspect of the subsequent commodification of human labor in both colonial and capitalist models and is responsible for the treatment of various groups of human beings *as* animals in a paradigm that denies alterity to the animal. While animals were killed for consumption in precolonial South Africa, "indigenous peoples actively fattened the land," practicing ecological conservatism, "rather than live off its fat" (Beinart and Coates 52). Clearly, a return to a precolonial agricultural model is unfeasible given the current South African sociopolitical and global context, but the ability for South African authors to imagine and depict different relationships with animals at least opens up a space in which one may imagine different relationships with other humans. Therefore, literature that depicts animals both as metaphors for human oppression of humans and as literal entities does extensive psychological work within the various interregnums of South African consciousness, pushing readers to try to imagine reciprocal relationships in ways that are not reductively construed as either black or white, animal or human.

For Coetzee, in the seemingly silent vacuum that constitutes the interregnum between recognition and action, that reciprocity begins with a voiceless enunciation, the greeting that can potentially take place between human and animal within any binary context that reinforces hierarchical ordering. Such a context designates animals inferior to humans and, alternately, renders specific humans inferior to others, not only within South Africa, but in all relationships that invite recognition of the self as distinct from another and that originate in a distinction between "nature" and "culture." The inability to see verisimilitude between nature and culture is highlighted in literary texts that represent the plight of one group of people at the hands of another by using the animal as a metaphor for the oppressed group. For example, the use of the animal as metaphor for subjected groups of individuals is prevalent in literature that explicates the plight of the oppressed, a fact that supports a reading of the animal body as the locus of oppositional thinking, the foundational example of all subsequent forms of human othering.[3] In such narratives, shared racial or ethnic pain, pain produced by relationships between masters and slaves, turns everyone into animals, but to draw such a correlation is to rely on a system of thought that refuses to acknowledge the animal as deserving of the same kinds of respect human beings *should* grant to other humans. In Coetzee's *The Lives of Animals*, when Abraham Stern calls into question Elizabeth Costello's claim that the meat industry in the West is analogous to the Holocaust, Coetzee deconstructs such binary thinking by exploring the philosophical implications of comparing human beings to animals specifically in terms of the Holocaust. Stern claims that "if Jews were treated like cattle, it does not follow that cattle are treated like Jews. The inversion insults the memory of the dead" (50). In this instance as in most others, despite the dialogic nature of Stern's comments, the animal metaphor is viewed as an insult rather than a plea for the disruption of dualistic thinking about humans and animals and, alternately, about certain groups of humans and other groups of humans.

In much South African literature, the animal is positioned within the context of the various aforementioned interregnums that characterize both South African literature and culture, the undefined historical and limnal moments that complicate the metaphor and serve to place the animal between the two orders defined by Gramsci and explicated by Gordimer, one present and one unforeseeable. In Olive Schreiner's *The Story of an African Farm* (1883), a novel that is a foundational influence on Coetzee's own treatment of the South African landscape,[4] Lyndall characterizes the role of the natural world—not the world constructed and ordered by humans—as the entity capable of action within an interregnum determined by a pronounced lack of equality for both colonized Africans and for women. Lyndall describes this space as indicative of the moment "when in the present there is no craving, and in the future no hope" (268). Like John's later claim in Coetzee's autobiographical *Boyhood*, that "*I belong to the farm*" (96), in the interregnum, the land and animals are granted a kind of agency, to own and to embrace—or to deny—human beings. The interregnum characterized by Schreiner is both feminist and anti-colonial, marked by Lyndall's quest for an impossible equality denied to her as a woman within the colonial context of nineteenth-century South Africa. Despite its feminist focus, Schreiner's novel has been criticized for its tendency to treat black South African characters as mere unnamed extras, a critique that Ruth First and Ann Scott defend as "the point of the colonial condition: Africans were so far outside white society that that in itself was a statement about it" (97). Shreiner's text does, however, use the animal body as a symbolic stand-in for the oppressive treatment of blacks by white South Africans: "the ox dies in the yoke beneath its master's whip; it turns anguish-filled eyes on the sunlight, but there is no sign of recompense to be made it. The black man is shot like a dog, and it goes well with the shooter" (114). Rhetorically, oxen, black men, and dogs occupy the same symbolic space in Schreiner's novel, the space of silence and subjection that the text ultimately critiques.

Clearly such comparisons do not equate black South Africans with animals as do those in Sarah Gertrude Millin's later novel, *God's Stepchildren* (1924) in which the Hottentots are described as "little yellow, monkey-like people" (17). Instead, Schreiner's narrator's comparison gives insight into the white South African tendency to categorize blacks as sub-human, as animal, and, therefore, as likely to receive the same treatment reserved for animals in a paradigm that designates animals as inferior to humans. Despite the fact that the above passage about the ox constitutes a clear critique of the dehumanization of the black Africans via the animal metaphor, what Schreiner's text does not do and, conversely, what Coetzee's narratives attempt, is to imagine a case for the disruption of the more originary dualism of animal and human. At the end of the narrative, after Lyndall's death, a death that could only take place during the interregnum where the intellect "look[s] back into the past; it [sees] the present; there [is] no future *now*" (252, my emphasis, Waldo reaches out to touch the chicks that run to their mother hen for protection. Only after he closes his eyes do the chicks approach him, climb upon him, and nestle into his clothing. While Em thinks that Waldo is sleeping and leaves his food for him to eat when he wakes, the novel ends with knowledge unavailable to humans who inhabit the interregnum; the chicks "kn[o]w better" (Schreiner 270) than Em that the future holds the possibility that Waldo, in fact, may never wake.

Schreiner, like Coetzee, writes outside of history, or, as Stephen Clingman claims, writes "another kind of history: one of the human soul, which it then projects onto the surrounding African landscape" (*Novels* 135). And Schreiner's landscape is in many ways a fiction, cut loose from some temporal historical narrative, a site of "wholesale absence," according to Coetzee, a "microcosm of colonial South Africa: a tiny community set down in the midst of the vastness of nature, living a close-minded and self-satisfied existence" (*White Writing* 64). Schreiner's novel serves to illustrate the ways that the animal as primary other signifies within the interregnum text. On Schreiner's African farm, certain animals are treated anthropomorphically—Waldo's dog Doss "wonders" (72) and has "tears in his eyes" (97)—in a move that, while sentimental, at least refuses to differentiate between animal and human behavior, thereby disrupting the animal and human dualism illustrated in Schreiner's linguistic comparison between the black man and the ox. In the narrative, Doss, as a named being, loves and receives love, dreams, and feels jealous. Conversely, the generic category of "dog" is also what Gregory refuses to be: "I will not be [Lyndall's] dog, and creep to *her* feet" (179). The dog that mediates the space between animal and human for Lyndall is a being that Lyndall accepts and allows to lick her hand, claiming, "where I do not love, I do not allow it" (199). But the dog is still viewed in a servile capacity—as a generality when read alongside the much more specific Doss—at least in the eyes of the white South African man exemplified by Gregory.

For Lyndall, the dog as domesticated companion, named pet, voiceless, living, and non-human constitutes the only site of possible connection within the interregnum and functions as the locus of mediation, the body that negotiates the space that distinguishes animal from human. In *The Companion Animal Manifesto: Dogs, People, and Significant Otherness*, Donna Haraway explores the complex relationship between dogs and humans claiming

> Dogs, in their historical complexity, matter here. Dogs are not an alibi
> for other themes; dogs are fleshly material-semiotic presences in the
> body of technoscience. Dogs are not surrogates for theory; they are not
> here just to think with. They are here to live with. Partners in the crime
> of human evolution, they are in the garden from the get-go, wily as
> Coyote. (5)

At least in the context of the dog/human companion species relationship, dogs occupy the same rhetorical space, according to Haraway, as humans; within this framework, then, it is worth noting that Doss has a more fully developed personality than any of the black characters in the novel, and, therefore, the status given to the dog is problematic. We can, however, read Doss as the one creature—aside from the chicks at the end of Schreiner's novel—capable of navigating the interregnum space and of disrupting the binaries between not only human and animal but also between living and dead. We can read Doss as a foil for Lyndall's stillborn child, a nameless, silent, human, and dead body that constitutes the seeming impossibility of an imagined future beyond the interregnum. The future is hopeless, stillborn in fact, for someone like Lyndall whose desire for female equality is deeply complicated by the layered inequities depicted on Schreiner's fictive South African farm.[5] Similarly, many of Coetzee's novels also contain dead or dying infants or references to the sterility of the historical moment as experienced through the bodies of the women who populate his texts.

For example, Susan Barton and Friday come across a dead baby by the side of the road in *Foe*, and Susan fears that Friday will revert to his former cannibalistic ways and eat the body (106); both the Magistrate in *Waiting for the Barbarians* and Michael in *Life & Times of Michael K* witness the deaths of two infants whose mothers are imprisoned in various camps (20 and 89, respectively). In *In the Heart of the Country*, Magda asks, "who would wake my slumbering eggs?" (10), and in *Age of Iron*, Elizabeth Curren proclaims that her cancer, like her womb, is "dry, bloodless, slow, and cold" (64). In these novels as in Schreiner's *The Story of an African Farm*, animals, dead children, or impossible pregnancies point to the seeming implausibility that anything can be "born" during the period of morbid symptoms that characterize South Africa's various interregnums. But these silent "characters" also signify within these texts by providing potential for possible transition: both dead bodies and animals are unspeaking, unable to provide a narrative of salvation, but, like the black body that will not stay buried and that rises to the earth's surface on Mehring's farm in Gordimer's *The Conservationist* (1972), the silent body's mere presence disrupts and complicates the narrative impulse to explain the colonial project or to provide a master narrative that in any way denies the presence of the subjugated and silenced body of the racialized other in South African literature. As Mehring realizes, the body of the other is "impossible to get rid of even by ordeal by fire" (110); through its refusal to stay buried, the body speaks for itself in spite of its silence.

Furthermore, in much South African literature, animals also "speak" a counter narrative to the predominant colonial mythology. For example, in Sol Plaatje's *Mhudi* (1930), the first novel written by a black South African, Mhudi's escape during the *Mfecane*, the conquering of the Nguni peoples by the Zulu early in the nineteenth century, is characterized by a return to the Edenic landscape, a natural world populated by animals and insects, bees who speak to Mhudi in "a familiar buzzing language" and "doves whose language [she] thought [she] could almost understand" (31). The interregnum depicted in Plaatje's novel is the moment between the *Mfecane* of the 1820s and 30s and the establishment of the Orange Free State and the South African Republic (eventually the Transvaal) later in the century. This moment is punctuated by Plaatje's fictional presentation of indigenous battles over land and animals, particularly the cattle that the narrator claims "seemed to take the situation mechanically as the ways of men and wars" (43). In South African literature, historically, the animal as simile shifts from comparisons of indigenous Africans to wild animals in the travel narratives of empire and early works of fiction by white South African authors—the monkey metaphor in Millin's narrative, for example—to more domesticated animals like dogs, oxen, and chickens in later works by both white and black authors. In Alan Paton's *Cry the Beloved Country* (1948), the simile in one instance is used to make a comparison between the suffering of animals, the suffering of women, and the suffering of blacks. When Stephen Kumalo's nameless wife sits "at his table, and put her head on it, and was silent, with the patient suffering of black women, with the suffering of oxen, with the suffering of any that are mute" (10), animal and woman are conflated in this representation of the silent and nameless suffering of all black South African peoples.

Similarly, in the 1950s South Africa depicted in Bloke Modisane's autobiographical *Blame Me on History* (1963), a girlfriend who works in a white household gives Modisane the meat prepared for the dogs "which were fed more nutritiously than the children of the locations" (56). After SPCA members see township dogs eat from latrines, the SPCA reacts by lobbying to restrict African pet ownership. In response, Modisane says, "it was easy for them to be publicly appalled, they did not have to live with it, they did not, as did the Africans, have to hate themselves for being unable to feed both the children and their dogs" (179). The animal as pet, like Doss in *Story of an African Farm*, is positioned in a place of privilege within white South African households, usurping the position of nameless black South Africans who suffer *like animals*. Such a paradigm highlights human need, but only in circumstances that perpetuate a hierarchical distinction between appropriate treatment for animals and humans. Nadine Gordimer reinforces the distinction between animal and human when she provides an explicit and powerful critique of the animal rights mentality in South Africa while simultaneously examining the hierarchical structure of the apartheid culture responsible for the mistreatment of animals by blacks and the elevation of specific animals by privileged whites. In *Burger's Daughter* (1979), Rosa Burger seemingly provides a direct reply to Bloke Modisane's statements about white attention to animals, specifically pets, when she claims anti-apartheid lawyer "Lionel [Burger] loved animals almost sentimentally" (196), something she refuses to do. When she sees a black man whipping a donkey, she sees not the whip but "the infliction of pain broken away from the will that creates it . . . pure cruelty gone beyond control of the humans who have spent thousands of years devising it" (208). Rosa will not, therefore, step between the man and the animal because such a gesture would negate the suffering of the man and shift the focus to the suffering of the animal.

Inherent in Modisane's autobiography as well as in Rosa Burger's fictional response to the man and the donkey is the overarching premise that before the animal can be liberated, humans must be liberated from the institutionalized racism of apartheid. To this way of thinking, the apartheid hierarchy that designates black Africans inferior to whites is an altogether separate entity from the hierarchy that designates humans superior to non-human animals; perhaps one of Coetzee's main fictional accomplishments is the attempt by many of his characters to imagine the negation of this extremely prevalent distinction. Modisane says, "the white man can take their South Africa and hand it back to the animals; perhaps they can find a way to live together under the will of a law which shall be acceptable to both: that the strong shall prey on the weak. Man has failed" (179). While Modisane clearly asserts the unwillingness of the native Africans to be further subjected by white rule, his suggestion, albeit ironic, would essentially replace one form of colonial domination with another without really changing the dualistic thinking responsible for the othering of indigenous South African peoples by whites. And such thinking is further perpetuated—or mimicked—in terms of literary representations of various hierarchical relationships between black South Africans.

For example, when Zani is stabbed by another black character in Njubulo Ndebele's "Fools" (1986), he becomes "like a chicken that's being slaughtered with a blunt knife. . . . He looked undignified. All the self-confidence, the self-assurance of that morning had evaporated. All the human attributes. And what was left was all animal" (181). Furthermore, when Mimi brings Zamini a chicken as a token of gratitude, he rapes her and then kills the chicken; the "fading cry" of the woman in the street is synonymous with the agony of the animal left to "flutter to death freely in the dark" (195). Underlying this scenario is a complex and multi-tiered system of oppression that can be read as it descends from white to black man to black woman to animal. Because of apartheid conceptions of self and other predicated on a more pervasive binary rhetoric, the black characters in Ndebele's story treat one another as animals as they continually reinscribe racialized distinctions onto other categories of difference based on such variables as gender, education level, and physical strength. In terms of these variables, the reinscription of the Xhosa cattle killing of 1856-57 as a trope in contemporary South African literature illustrates its function as a signifier of such multi-faceted displacements.

The legacy of the cattle killing as an act of resistance is felt profoundly in contemporary South African fiction like Sindiwe Magona's *Mother to Mother* (1998) and Zakes Mda's *Heart of Redness* (2000). In *Mother to Mother*, Mandisa's grandfather describes the deep resentment that must have driven the Xhosa to kill their cattle, a resentment that in his retelling of the oral narrative of the Xhosa history marks the cattle killing as an act of extreme bravery as opposed to the act of ignorance and superstition described by Mandisa's white teachers. In Magona's narrative, the incident of the killing and its presentation within the context of codified, white-authored South African history provides an example of the ways that whites, both historically and in the current moment, manipulate colonial history at the expense of indigenous oral narrative. Magona's novel, in an ironic turn, transcribes the oral history of the cattle killing in an attempt to voice the Xhosa side of the story. Mandisa's grandfather tells her that cattle are not merely food but serve a much more foundational and holistic function in Xhosa culture as the source of milk, dung, and clothing, and that to kill such an esteemed creature was a hugely significant phenomenon. He says that the sacrifice of the cattle and crops "was to drive abelungu [whites] to the sea, where, so the seer had said, they would all drown . . . . Such noble sacrifice. But then, the more terrible the abomination, the greater the sacrifice called for" (178).

Similarly, in *Heart of Redness*, Zakes Mda illustrates the divide and conquer strategy employed by the British colonizers who viewed the native Africans as vermin. The Great White Chief claims, "extermination is now the only word and principle that guides us. I loved these people and considered them my children. But now I say exterminate the savage beasts" (19). Such an indictment points to the cognitive leap from "children" to "beasts" that is easily made within the hierarchical mentality that defined the colonial milieu, a mentality in transition between 1811 and 1855 when "the African went, in British eyes, from noble savage awaiting religious and economic conversion to 'irreclaimable'" (Ohlson and Stedman 24). In Mda's novel, after Nongqawuse delivers her prophetic message, the Xhosa turn against one another as Unbelievers and Believers argue over the truth of the prophecy, and Mda juxtaposes this historical event against a battle over whether or not to build a casino in Qolorha 150 years later. Like Magona's novel, Mda's narrative makes a case for Nongqawuse and her followers when Camagu says, "what I am saying is that it is wrong to dismiss those who believed in Nongqawuse as foolish . . . . Her prophecies arose out of the spiritual and mental anguish of the amaXhosa nation" (245) as a result of its treatment at the hands of whites. Mda's novel explores the ways that the prophecy was founded on a hierarchical system of scapegoating and displacement: just as the British mentality rendered the Xhosa "savage beasts," the Xhosa, in turn, killed their cattle, and, in Mda's narrative, for generations after the killing the Believers scapegoat the Unbelievers and vice versa in seemingly endless self-defeating mimicry of the colonial project.

While the nature of this scapegoat mentality is not dependent upon a colonial infrastructure, it is impossible to read the scapegoat narrative of the cattle killing outside of the colonial situation imposed on the Xhosa. The destruction of crops and animals is clearly indicative of mentalities in transition; physically powerless against the British colonizers, the Xhosa displaced their aggression onto entities that they constructed as other for perhaps the first time in their history: animals and the land. The fact that the death of the cattle and destruction of the crops was intended to bring about the regeneration of plants, animals, *and* humans points to an attempt to restore a more interdependent and holistic order while abolishing the colonial imperative toward dualistic thinking. The cattle killing was an effort to preempt colonial rule instead of seeking to progress by colonial standards and engaging in the capitalist exchange of currency, the "button without a hole" (Magona 182) described by Mandisa's grandfather. As such and because Xhosa action was displaced onto the animal body as symbolic sacrifice, the goal of the movement, to drive the whites from South Africa, failed.

As a result of the pervasive starvation that followed the cattle killing, the Xhosa stole and ate horse meal from East London farms, and they also stole and ate the well-fed dogs of white settlers. In the most extreme cases, there is evidence to suggest that they were even driven to devour their own children (Peires 242). Such is the equalizing power of starvation as described by Nadine Gordimer's narrator in *A Sport of Nature* (1987): "when you see everything reduced to hunger, nothing, nothing but the terrible way eyes look at you, men, women, children, cattle, dogs—the eyes become the same—you can't remember anything else" (268). In an unpublished paper, Elleke Boehmer argues that in *Disgrace* Coetzee reestablishes the parochial practice of scapegoating in a secular society ("Sorry, Sorrier, Sorriest"), and I would further this stance by claiming that many of the underlying beliefs of a particular scapegoat situation, the Xhosa cattle killing, are present in *Disgrace* as well. A chief difference between the two instances, one historical and one a work of fiction, is that while the Xhosa established binary distinctions by killing cattle that were essential for the survival of the Xhosa, the characters in Coetzee's novel seek to undo those distinctions by caring for and euthanizing the "superfluous" pet population of South Africa.

Furthermore, in *Disgrace* Coetzee rewrites the "ending" for both Olive Schreiner and Lyndall—as well as for much of the literature that I have discussed in this chapter thus far—by inverting the significations of animal and child: the narrative closes with David Lurie's sense of calling and responsibility for the corpses of euthanized, unwanted dogs and with Lucy Lurie's claim of responsibility for *her* unborn child, the product of a violent rape. In *Disgrace*, unlike *The Story of an African Farm*, the existence of the yet unborn human and the claim of responsibility for the body of the other—even if the body is that of a dog, and, furthermore, the body of a dead dog—provide hope for moving beyond the interregnum "now" and establish the potential for reciprocity. The dog that David decides to euthanize at the end of *Disgrace*, like Doss in *The Story of an African Farm*, is sentimentalized, presented to the reader as a sacrificial lamb. David Lurie opens the dog's cage and beckons to the animal: "the dog wags its crippled rear, sniffs [David's] face, licks his cheeks, his lips, his ears. He does nothing to stop it" (220). To claim that Coetzee's writing is sentimental is to do something taboo, to equate Coetzee's austere prose with womanish effusiveness—a point that becomes increasingly contentious in terms of later academic and critical responses to Coetzee's female alter-ego, the title character of *Elizabeth Costello* (2003). But such a claim also makes an unusual case for the overtly political in Coetzee's writing, as social movements are often founded on sentiment.[6] The animal, like Lyndall and her unborn child in Schreiner's narrative, becomes the sacrificial offering to the machine of colonial and capitalist modernity.

* * *

When Anne Susskind asked Coetzee if he liked animals better than people, he answered by saying, "my fundamental relation with living beings is not one of liking versus disliking. What is my fundamental relation? A hard question. Perhaps a relation of greeting. How do I greet this being with whom I share life? How does this being greet me?" ("The Émigré"). In Coetzee's fiction, the animals that human characters must greet are, by and large, dogs. According to Boria Sax, "in Eurasia around 12,000 B.C.—or much earlier, according to some theorists—the dog became the first animal to be domesticated by human beings" (85). Even before its domestication and certainly since then, the dog has been a predominant figure in world mythology, primarily as a boundary keeper between the realms of life and death. For example, in Egyptian mythology, dogs are associated with Anubis, the god of the dead, and in Greco-Roman mythology, the dog Cerebus stands at the gates of Hades. Historically, dogs as domesticated animals also function as boundary keepers, bridging the gap between the binary oppositions of nature and culture, just as they function mythologically to negotiate the oppositional realms of life and death. Despite the fact that, according to Mary Elizabeth Thurston, "duality weaves through the history of canine culture . . . with dogs perceived as exploitable tools and, often at the same time, as intimate friends" (268), the dog's ability to mediate oppositions—masculine/feminine, living/dead, domesticated/wild—problematizes the set of human emotions that we are "supposed" to feel towards animals as lesser beings; conversely, we "view dogs with a strange combination of affection and contempt, of domination and fear" (Sax 86). In Coetzee's work, dogs serve similar mediating functions and are treated with similar ambiguity; as both symbol and speechless body, the dog inhabits the taboo and unspeakable regions of oppositional thought to disrupt dichotomous categories such as colonizer/colonized, human/animal, and, ultimately, self/other. The voiceless dog, as representative of absolute alterity—that which evades attempts at imagined identification—in Coetzee's work, becomes a pivot around which altruistic ethical action is centered. Because we have no access to the interiority of the dog, human response to canine suffering must be based on reasons other than the dog's ability to express gratitude or to ask for help.

As I have stated previously, the animal as literary icon permeates South African literature, and I am not the first literary critic to read the animal within the South African text. In "Nadine Gordimer: A Writing Life," Stephen Clingman playfully attempts to flesh out the "essential, underlying matrix—the DNA, as it were, of Gordimer's fiction" (6) by examining the role of another domesticated animal, the cat, in Gordimer's work. Gordimer's own self-portrait, in fact, is a cat from two perspectives, one facing forward, one facing away.[7] Clingman examines the "doubleness of cats" in Gordimer's work by describing the ways that cats respect no recognized boundaries. He says

> It is no accident that . . . a cat appears when Hillela [in *A Sport of Nature*] is making love, for Hillela is Gordimer's most feline of creatures, with a bodily sensuality that knows no conventional social bounds. On the one hand, this is an amoral if not anti-moral body, going where it pleases, unpredictable and therefore dangerous. Yet in the context of an apartheid world, this disposition also means that Hillela will not conform to any of the arbitrary limits of race . . . . Hers is an essential liberation of the body, and a fusion between mind and body: exactly what the sensuality of a cat suggests. (8)

In Gordimer's work, it seems, the feline body functions in part as a reflection of the female body, of the strength of Gordimer's heroines, and of their refusal to ascribe to a set of proscriptions that undermines the decisions enacted by the body. Furthermore, the cat as voiceless body acts instead of speaking (or writing) and provides a critique of physical actions that subvert codified norms, specifically the decision of whites to work against apartheid, or, read another way, the decision of women to embrace the bodily over the rational, to let the decisions of the body work out the problems of history.

In discussing dogs in Coetzee's work, I do not want to get into an essentializing discourse, to say that women are like cats and men are like dogs, or, more specifically, that Gordimer is like a cat and Coetzee like a dog, but it is easy to see how such a reading might occur, especially considering the degree to which Coetzee's implicit ethics are held up for critical comparison alongside Gordimer's explicit politics. It is tempting to see another Coetzee/Gordimer binary taking shape by including such an analysis, but I would tend to argue that the prevalence of the animal in the works of both authors—and perhaps more generally within South African literature—speaks to larger issues of representation and embodiment within a socio-historical framework markedly shaped by an extremely problematic relationship between self and other. The cat disengages and breaks the rules; it has the choice to do so. Conversely, the dog seeks nothing other than to engage and is completely dependent on human whim to fulfill or deny that interaction. When Coetzee writes about dogs, or when he claims that someone is "like a dog"—one of the most frequently occurring phrases in Coetzee's corpus—he is saying something about all bodies, about a body's placement in a system of oppression. That body may be male or female, black or white, or in may, in fact, be animal, the body that maintains its silent knowledge of the interregnum, representing nothing except itself and our human ability, our power, to relieve it from or to abandon it to suffering.

In his fiction, Coetzee makes clear the connection between the destruction of animals and the othering of human beings, including white women and indigenous Africans, an othering that theoretically began with the historical shift from nomadic, hunter/gatherer societies to agriculturally-based societies indicative of the beginnings of "culture." According to Charles Patterson, the domestication of animals that took place after this shift "affected the way humans related to their captive animals and in turn to each other" (10) by causing humans to establish a myth of their own superiority, a myth that is fully explored in Coetzee's first work of fiction *Dusklands*, particularly in "The Narrative of Jacobus Coetzee," the fictional account of Boer expansion in 1760 that comprises the second half of this work. In this novella, Jacobus claims that Bushman women are tied to nothing because they have seen their men "shot down like dogs" (61). By aligning the native South African peoples with animals—as Jacobus claims, "death is as obscure to [the bushman] as to an animal" (80)—they obviously become easier to kill. By subscribing to such logic, Jacobus articulates an enabling myth of his own superiority over the indigenous people that he kills, a narrative based upon a fable he tells himself about an actual animal, the hare:

> The death of the hare is the logic of salvation. For either he was living
> out there and is dying into a world of objects, and I am content; or he
> was living within me and would not die within me, for we know that no
> man ever yet hated his own flesh, that flesh will not kill itself, that every

suicide is a declaration of the otherness of killer from victim. The death of the hare is my metaphysical meat, just as the hare is the meat of my dogs. The hare dies to keep my soul from merging with the world. All honour to the hare. (80)

Jacobus's sentiment about the hare also applies to the big game that he hunts as he treks into the South African interior, game that ultimately includes the indigenous South African peoples he rhetorically constructs as animals, kills and, on some metaphorical level, devours.

"The Narrative of Jacobus Coetzee" purports to be J. M. Coetzee's translation of both "the Dutch of Jacobus Coetzee's narrative and the Afrikaans of [his] father's [Dr. S. J. Coetzee] Introduction" (55) to a previous volume. The primary text consists of the translator's note followed by a first-person account of Jacobus's two journeys across the Great River into the land of the Great Namaqua. The purpose of the first trek is to hunt elephants, and the goal of the second is not only to kill the servants who abandon Jacobus on his previous journey, but also to annihilate the Namaqua camp and all of its inhabitants. The chronicle of these sojourns is followed by S. J. Coetzee's afterword that "ventures to present a more complete and therefore more just view of Jacobus Coetzee. It is a work of piety but also a work of history" (108). This "document" names Jacobus as not only the discoverer of the Orange River but also of the giraffe (108) and includes no information about the second journey whatsoever because the narrator characterizes the events of the second journey as superfluous, claiming that "man's thrust into the future is history; all the rest, the dallying by the wayside, the retraced path, belongs to anecdote, the evening by the hearth fire" (121). The afterword is followed by a deposition made by Jacobus in 1760, the only authentic historical document among the various others that J. M. Coetzee presents as real. The act of reading these supposed historical documents—rearranged (J. M. Coetzee claims that the afterword in this text constitutes the introduction in his father's) and contradictory—serves to alienate the reader from any recognizable distinction between truth and lie, history and fiction. Furthermore, the multiplicity of subjectivities that inhabit these various documents—J. M. Coetzee, S. J. Coetzee, Jacobus Coetzee, and Rijk Tulbagh (who transcribes the deposition that constitutes the appendix)—engage in a dialogue with one another that ultimately debunks both the enabling myth that allows for colonial domination and the fable through which Jacobus asserts his distinctness from the hare, the fable that in turn allows him to treat indigenous South Africans as animals and, more disturbingly, as meat.

On the one hand, J. M. Coetzee's project can be read, as Sheila Collingwood-Whittick does, as a critique of recorded South African history. She claims that Coetzee's narrative reveals "the flagrant contradiction that exists between what is chronicled, alleged or transmitted through the annals of South African history and the reality concealed behind the facade of that hectoring discourse" ("J. M. Coetzee's *Dusklands*" 75). But through various alienation effects that keep the reader from being able to willingly suspend disbelief and buy, wholesale, the fiction of history, the narrative also provides a critique of all codified discourse, fictional or historical, South African or otherwise. In Brechtian epic theater, such alienation effects turn the specta- tor—one who stands outside and watches—into an observer—one who has a capacity for action and a moral imperative to make decisions (Brecht 37). The complete text of *Dusklands* with its "many narrators (the various parts of the two novellas have at least three primary narrative voices, plus a whole chorus of secondary voices who affect the telling of the stories)" (Maus 205) situates "The Vietnam Project" before Jacobus's narrative—a narrative that takes place two hundred years before the Vietnamese War chronicled in the preceding novella. Such arrangement, as Vicki Briault Manus claims, with its "idiosyncratic style and other anachronisms" ("The Colonialist Subject" 42) further destabilizes readings of time and place as do Jacobus's various narra- tive inconsistencies (for example, he provides two differing accounts of his servant Klawer's fate: in one, Klawer is swept away in the river; in the other, Klawer grows ill and asks Jacobus to leave him (94-95)).

The audience is made further suspicious by S. J. Coetzee's third-person narrative certainty in the afterword—"[Jacobus] Coetzee glanced neither right nor left as he passed through the defiles of the Khamies mountains" (118)—juxtaposed with narrative speculation in the same section of the text: after discovering the river, "here he *might* have rested all day" (120, my emphasis). By the time the reader encounters the list of bodily minutiae left by Jacobus's party, items including ear wax, semen, and kidney stones (119), it is impossible not to be incredulous. Furthermore, there can be no doubt that if one believes the first account—Jacobus's account—then one cannot believe the second and vice versa; the various narratives, therefore, cancel the veracity of one another. Perhaps the most significant result of these various alienation effects is the displacement of the enabling myth that allows for colonization, the belief stated with suspicious ease and articulate self-aware- ness by Jacobus that the indigenous people are animals. According to Shelia Collingwood-Whittick, "if, as the myth proposes, the colonist is dealing with an animal or thing, he cannot be expected to act or react with the same sense of moral responsibility that would normally determine the conduct of one human being towards another" ("J. M. Coetzee's *Dusklands*" 81). When taken as one element on a continuum of binary thought, the problem with Jacobus's mythological thinking about humans as animals and the problem that Coetzee's writing exposes is not so much that Jacobus equates Africans with animals, but that he equates animals with things; in order for this sort of justification to operate in the colonial model, before it becomes theoretically acceptable to kill an African because he is a dog, it must first be acceptable to kill a dog (or an elephant or a giraffe) because she or he is an object.

While elephants, giraffes and hares—all of which Jacobus kills—are present in the text, the literal body of the dog is absent from Jacobus's narrative, but the simile has the power to justify Jacobus's destruction of the native South Africans. When Jacobus kills his former servant Plaatje, he claims that Plaatje's "eyes apologized like a dog's" (103). The dog simile that recurs in *Dusklands* as a linguistic device for othering the native Africans is juxtaposed against descriptions of the animals that inhabit the South African landscape, the cattle, giraffes, hippopotami, and elephants, as well as the "metaphysical" hare. Furthermore, Jacobus's ability to destroy living beings, animal or human, establishes his difference from those beings that cannot destroy him and enforces binary thinking about the distinction between life and death. For example, Jacobus describes the role of the gun in the dualistic endeavor of empire: "the gun saves us from the fear that all life is within us," and its use is Jacobus's "incessant proclamation of the otherness of the dead and therefore the otherness of life." In this context, according to Jacobus, arises the fable of human superiority: "the death of the hare is [his] metaphysical meat" (79).

The animal body becomes the primary site of an othering justified by its construction not only as meat—thing, sustenance, consumable object— but also as dead and ultimately as sacrificial, linguistic, "metaphysical" enabler. As I stated in my introduction, Carol J. Adams claims that animals become "absent referents" (40) when they are butchered because linguistically, they are rendered nonentities: the term "meat" implies thingness, further negating the need for ethics in the realm of animals and, by extension, any human associated with animals. It is not surprising then that Jacobus essentially turns an African child into meat when he bites off the child's ear (90). Consumption of meat and ultimately of the child whose body has no more status than meat becomes a metaphor for the destruction that is part and parcel of the colonial project, the means by which the colonialist's self is extracted from an unfamiliar landscape in the mythological establishment of "order." During his quest into the interior, Jacobus moves through "the land cutting a devouring path from horizon to horizon" (79), essentially mapping and ordering the nameless wilderness of incomprehensibility before him, a mapping that Coetzee renders through a rhetoric of consumption: Jacobus's symbolic devouring of the land parallels his more disturbingly literal consumption and ingestion of its animal and human inhabitants.

The hunger characterized by this passage is the inverse of that which rendered all beings equal during the starvation that followed the Xhosa cattle killing; by contrast, the white settler's hunger is fed by his destruction and consumption of the South African landscape, animals, and people that constitute both "metaphysical" and literal meat. As a hunter, Jacobus travels into the interior to hunt elephants and to explore territory that was unexplored by white colonists in the 1700s.[8] Collingwood-Whittick claims that the Dutch colonialists needed to secure and maintain a morally tenable position for themselves in a situation where "the landscapes, the climate, the flora and fauna and, most threateningly, the indigenous inhabitants" ("J. M. Coetzee's" 75) were aberrant to them. Furthermore, the tendency by colonizers to view various peoples as animals follows the phallocentric goal of colonization, to dominate and control the land, which is feminine and passive in the rhetoric of Western philosophy that is foundational to the discourse of empire. For example, in the other novella that accompanies Jacobus's narrative in *Dusklands*, "The Vietnam Project," Eugene Dawn describes how "we live no longer by tilling the earth but by devouring her"(26), just as Jacobus cuts a "devouring path" into the South African interior. When the land is viewed as a consumable object, the people that populate the land are rendered fair game, and under the auspices of colonization, both land and inhabitants are feminized. Of "The Narrative of Jacobus Coetzee," Vicki Briault Manus claims, "it is hard to believe that [Jacobus] is referring to people, and not to animals" (44), but in the eyes of the Boer explorer, the indigenous Africans do not constitute another order of human being; they are something subhuman and therefore negligible, merely a lesser entity in the mythical food chain that begins with the earth and ends with white men.[9]

References to Jacobus's indifference to the loss of animal and indigenous African life abound within the narrative of his journeys that begin with the hunting of a bushman who, according to Jacobus, "is a different creature, a wild animal with an animal's soul" (58) and ends with his claim that "like God in a whirlwind I fell upon a lamb . . . and slit his throat" (100). During his second journey, the myth and Jacobus's ability to think of himself as God extend not only to the bushmen but also to the servants who abandon him after his first journey. After he kills a young girl with "a shot, one of the simple, matter-of-fact kind" (100), he again conflates animal and human by saying, "like the sparrow, you are not forgotten" (101) before he kills his former servants. Jacobus's narrative ends with the declamation that the people he has killed now function in the fabulary position of the hare: "through their deaths I, who . . . had wandered the desert like a pallid symbol, again asserted my reality" (106). Jacobus's final sentiment could well be J. M. Coetzee's commentary about both the nature of imagined identification as well as about his own resistance to voicing the other in his fiction. Jacobus says,

> I too can attain and inhabit a point of view from which, like Plaatje, like Adonis, like Tamboer & Tamboer, like the Namaqua, I can be seen as superfluous. At present I do not care to inhabit such a point of view; but when the day comes you will find that whether I am alive or dead, whether I ever lived or was never born, has never been of real concern to me. (107)

These final sentiments do several things in the service of destabilizing both text and audience. First, by naming all of the men that Jacobus has killed, Coetzee—via Jacobus—assures that they are not superfluous to the narrative despite the fact that they remain largely silent within the text. Second, Jacobus seemingly speaks to S. J. Coetzee who claims "to understand the life of this obscure farmer requires a positive act of the imagination" (109). Both Jacobus's and S. J. Coetzee's sentiments indicate that it is possible to imagine the interiority of the other, whether that other is a black South African or an eighteenth-century Boer farmer. But, as the various subjectivities that dialogue in "The Narrative of Jacobus Coetzee" make clear, the ability to imagine depends upon recorded or spoken "truth;" we may be able to "imagine" being Jacobus just as Jacobus can "inhabit" the point of view of Plaatje, but in both instances, we will be less than accurate in our assumed identification, our enactment and mimicry of an unknowable interiority.

The various tropes that Coetzee introduces in *Dusklands*—the destabilization of an enabling colonial mythology, a critique of imagined identification, the interplay of multiple narrative subjectivities, and the originary and binary logic inherent in the fable of the hare—underlie his subsequent body of work. The assertion of human superiority in any agricultural social framework is followed by further distinctions between various groups of peoples and between the practices associated with those groups. The ability to control animals is essentially the way that humans learned to control other humans; furthermore, control of animals contributes to the gendered binary logic inherent in Western culture that establishes the existence of various others and is based on a superior male, inferior female model. According to Greta Gaard, the way that women and nature have been conceptualized in the West "has resulted in devaluing whatever is associated with women, emotion, animals, and nature, while simultaneously elevating in value those things associated with men, reason, humans, culture, and the mind" (5). Along with the function of the animal within the interregnum, Coetzee uses the animal as linguistic phenomenon, as simile, to illustrate the plight of women, native Africans, and, ultimately, in a typically Hegelian way, white men within any framework in which the master/slave model is operative. According to Greta Gaard, "not only is [English] male-centered, it is human-centered as well" (64). As such, the animal simile arises as a way not only to ascribe inferior status to people who are by extension treated "like" animals—white women and native Africans, for example—but to emasculate male subjects who shift back and forth between othering and othered in the colonial model.

Coetzee's examination of the role of gender in the animal/human equation is particularly apparent in *In the Heart of the Country* (1977) and *Waiting for the Barbarians* (1980). The prevalence of the dog as simile appears in *In the Heart of the Country* when Magda's father bribes his servant Hendrik with alcohol so that he can sleep with Hendrik's wife Anna. Magda later hears Hendrik making "the sound of a distempered dog whining and growling and panting without cease" (60). Magda's father placates his black servant whom he views as subhuman animal and then sleeps with Anna whom he views as consumable property, like the land from which he has displaced her. According to Lori Gruen, "the categories 'woman' and 'animal' serve the same symbolic function in patriarchal society" (61), but such a claim is problematized in the colonial situation where colonized males are also alternately feminized and rendered animal; the criteria that establish the opposition of ruled and ruling, dog and human, man and woman remain in a state of flux as long as the colonial model stays in place. For example, in *Waiting for the Barbarians*, the Magistrate conflates the categories of woman and animal when he refers to both a fox cub and a barbarian girl as "wild animals" (35). Later, however, the paradigm shifts after the Magistrate voices his opposition to the physical torture enacted on the "barbarian" prisoners by Colonel Joll. The Magistrate is forced to wear a dress while he is tortured by Joll's men, and it is in the uncertain relationship between oppressor and oppressed that human and animal, female and male dichotomies are revealed as essentially unstable. The Magistrate is forced to occupy not only the position of animal, the man who "licked his food off the flagstones like a dog" (124), the man who ultimately believes that "there is no way of dying allowed [him], it seems, except like a dog in a corner" (117), but is also forced to signify as a woman. His status as benevolent colonizer has been subverted, and by the time he realizes that through his less physically violent actions he seeks the same confession that Joll seeks through torture, he is placed in the position of emasculated victim to the violent whims of the more overtly brutal colonial regime.

In *Age of Iron* (1990), the position of the dog shifts from simile to symbol. When Elizabeth Curren lets the vagabond Vercueil into her home, he is followed by a dog, "a collie, young, little more than a pup" (6). In writing the letter to her daughter that she never sends, Elizabeth Curren asks, "why do I give this man food? For the same reason I would feed his dog (stolen, I am sure) if it came begging. For the same reason I gave you my breast" (7). The animal as pet, the dog cared for by Vercueil, serves as a symbol for Elizabeth's own treatment of Vercueil himself as well as her subsequent treatment of her black housekeeper, Florence. Elizabeth treats Vercueil the way he treats the dog, like a pet, and imagines herself searching for him, "calling softly, 'Mr. Vercueil! Mr. Vercueil!' An old woman in search of her cat" (48). Her assumption that the dog is stolen negates the possibility of free will for the dog and, instead, the dog becomes a victim of colonial appropriation, the recipient of Vercueil's paternalism: the dog lives at the whim of Vercueil, just as Elizabeth Curren's seemingly boundless giving is also a whim, checked when it comes to the black South Africans whose land she has, by virtue of her heritage, stolen from them. Despite the fact that she is willing to admit the catlike, reticent, and disdainful Vercueil into her home, Elizabeth is unable to recognize the black South Africans, in the form of Florence and her children, as members of her family.

When a black township boy named John comes to stay with Florence's son Bheki, for example, Elizabeth protests by claiming that she cannot give shelter to every township child in need (54). Elizabeth may realize Derrida's claim that "the demands of the other are infinite" (Attridge, "Expecting" 31), that she must pick and choose among them, but her choice of allowing Vercueil instead of John into her home is based on a symbolic need to care for a silent pet, and by extension, to care for her absent and silent daughter. Her inability to see the connections between dog, white man, black township child, and her own daughter ultimately causes her to misread her dream of Florence as a goddess, ascribing to her housekeeper the wrong attributes, those of classical literature instead of those from a South African mythology that Elizabeth, for all of her education, has failed to learn. When Mr. Thabane directs Elizabeth to leave the township, he tells her to follow the "signs to civilization" (107), but she gets lost. By believing in the figurative instead of the literal, by looking for the wrong set of signs and by ascribing symbolic status to Florence, to Vercueil and by extension, to his dog, Elizabeth misses the opportunity to destroy the boundaries that separate black from white and human from animal, United States citizen from South African, and adult from child. Of her dream of Florence, she says, "forever the goddess is passing, forever caught in a posture of surprise and regret, I do not follow" (178). In the interregnum depicted in *Age of Iron*, God is absent, and the only set of signs that can be deciphered are physical: the animal, the dead, and the landscape, all of which constitute a return of the repressed—in this case, a return of the feminine denied by the valorization of the masculine rhetoric of Western philosophical thought.

Such a female figure could be the "Mother of God" that Sergei Nechaev describes in *The Master of Petersburg* (1994), the entity that will come when the interregnum is over, "on the day after the last day . . . and make a pilgrimage to hell to plead for the damned" (201). In their attempts to decipher their own actions and to make sense of the existential reality of the various landscapes that they inhabit, landscapes always filled with images of war, Coetzee's characters seek signs, messages from God, the sky, and the spirits of the dead, and in turn always miss the obvious: the fact that there is no supernatural message, no *arrivant* in Derrida's sense,[10] that God is not salvation, that, quite possibly, there is no God. *The Master of Petersburg* is a narrative that brings to the forefront the existential quest for signs—the waiting for a specific calling—that functions as more of an undercurrent than a major trope in Coetzee's previous fiction.[11] Furthermore, the connection between the quest for signs and viewing the animal as symbol is intimately related. If one is always waiting to see signs, one may miss the opportunity to act in terms of the immediate, and the animal runs the risk of always being viewed as a sign; the dog may continually be viewed as metaphorical in a context that does not recognize as legitimate the interstitial spaces between the binary oppositions of animal and human, a context in which there is no respect for the alterity of the animal.

As is the case with "The Narrative of Jacobus Coetzee," the impetus for *The Master of Petersburg* is also based on a "true" story, the life of Russian author Fyodor Mikhailovich Dostoevsky. The narrative takes place in 1869 and begins with Dostoevsky's incognito journey from Dresden to St. Petersburg to collect the personal effects of his stepson, Pavel Isaev, who may have committed suicide but was more likely murdered by the police because of his participation in the nihilist operation led by Sergei Nechaev. Instead of leaving Petersburg—the logical thing to do since he is wanted by creditors—Dostoevsky waits for something, some sort of sign or signal, which ultimately arrives in the form of inspiration for his novel *The Devils*. He moves into Pavel's rooms and between episodes of epilepsy, begins alternately having an affair with the landlady, Anna Sergeyevna Kolenkina, and feeling desire for her adolescent daughter, Matryona/Matryosha. He also meets Nechaev and engages him in debates concerning the relationship of the artist to political activism, denouncing Nechaev's revolutionary stance. In *The Master of Petersburg*, Coetzee employs a third-person narrator, and according to Derek Attridge, "Coetzee has chosen . . . to view revolutionary activism through the eyes of a dedicated conservative" (26), a narrative choice that once again put Coetzee at odds with his critics, especially his fellow South Africans who had long accused him of refusing to engage in politics and who read *The Master of Petersburg* eager for evidence of their recent political triumph over apartheid. In many ways, the fictional Dostoevsky created by Coetzee stays very close to the historical Dostoevsky, a literary figure about whose work and life Coetzee has read and written a great deal.[12] But, as Derek Attridge claims, "the basic premise on which the novel is built—Dostoevsky coming to terms with Pavel's death—is glaringly contrafactual" ("Expecting" 25); in reality, Pavel outlived his stepfather and was neither murdered nor committed suicide.

The Master of Petersburg is very explicit in its treatment of the connection between the quest for signs and the tendency to deny alterity to animals and, by extension, to other humans. The novel is more replete with metaphorical and literal dogs than any of Coetzee's other novels: within the first seventeen pages, Dostoevsky goes to the "Isle of dogs" where his son is buried and where he sees "a dog, grey and emaciated" (2); Matryona inspects Dostoevsky "as a dog inspects a stranger" (14); and Dostoevsky believes he is not a poet but is "more like a dog that has lost its bone, scratching here, scratching there" (17). Later, he claims that grief is "a big grey dog, blind and deaf and stupid and immovable" (52). Like many of Coetzee's other characters, Dostoevsky seeks signs after the death of his stepson, Pavel. Instead, he finds only another dog abandoned in the night. In a moment that harkens back to Elizabeth Curren's relationship with Vercueil and his dog, Fyodor thinks, "is this what I will be doing for the rest of my days, peering into the eyes of dogs and beggars?" (81), but unlike Elizabeth Curren who takes in the beggar and his dog, Dostoevsky leaves the dog tied in the cold. In *The Master of Petersburg*, the dog fully shifts from symbol to literal entity, but Dostoevsky refuses to acknowledge the dog's alterity until it is too late, until he has left it, most likely, to freeze to death. Having decided that unless this dog is the esoteric sign that he is expecting, Dostoevsky chooses instead to wait for that which may never come.

Despite his subsequent realization that the dog might be "the least thing" (82), the first step towards establishing some connection with the world he searches for signs, he does not act to help it and cannot let go of his quest for external meaning. His actions after he encounters this dog are based on a fable like the myth of the hare that informs Jacobus's murderous trek in *Dusklands*, a fable that asserts the distinction between human and animal, that which can give aid and that which cannot ask for it: the narrator claims that Dostoevsky "is waiting for a sign, and he is betting . . . that the dog is not the sign at all, is just a dog among many dogs howling in the night" (83). Such thinking could be redeemed by his realization that "as long as he tries to distinguish things that are things from things that are signs he will not be saved" (83), but instead of saving the dog, he invites Ivanov Pyotr Alexandrovich—a spy in the guise of a beggar—into his rooms. Such "charity" is essentially self-serving, the product of a desire to "*expect the one [he does] not expect*" (84), and Dostoevsky regrets his invitation almost as soon as he extends it, realizing that whatever he hoped to attain by virtue of this gesture will not be forthcoming. His son will not come back to him, and he has missed the chance to save something, to relieve the suffering of the animal in his midst.

According to Derek Attridge, Dostoevsky is waiting for the *arrivant*, the unexpected, but Attridge claims that

> the cry of the dog . . . is not the unexpected . . . , it is the event that disrupts the order of the familiar with absolute heterogeneity, an appeal from the other which comes outside any structure of ethical obligation . . . . It is the easiest thing in the world to ignore. This is why it must be answered. ("Expecting" 29)

Attridge is wrong, however, if we consider an ethical structure that subverts models of dualistic thinking, a model that is outside of the binary camp, that which Michael K seeks to express. Dostoevsky realizes too late that metaphors are "nonsense," that "there is death, only death. Death is a metaphor for nothing. Death is death" (118), and the dog is a dog, deserving of salvation in its own right. As Rachael Lawlan claims, "at the end of the novel, Fyodor finds that there is no absolution, only make-believe resurrection" (152); perhaps this "make-believe" is hopeful, the preemptive moment that is neither absolution nor condemnation, the moment when Pavel signifies for his father as dead and as dead allows the father to move beyond the kind of thinking that designates a thing or being as sign or non-sign. If we are to believe Dostoevsky's statement about death, and I assert that his claim is also Coetzee's position—

that in order for reciprocity to find footing and in order for the master/slave dynamic to be disrupted, then we must forgo the quest for signs and react to the call of the dog in the snow—then the dog must ultimately be recognized and validated not for its power as simile or symbol, but as a being who suffers unjustly and to whom we owe some measure of ethical responsibility.

When Dostoevsky imagines Matryona in the throes of sexual ecstasy, the narrator claims that "his imagination seems to have no bounds" (76). This portrait of Dostoevsky is an unflattering examination of the creative imagination, the prurient as opposed to inspired sensibility that informs the writing of fiction. In fact, what ultimately disturbs Derek Attridge about the novel is that

> it presents a vision of the writing process, and more generally of creativity . . . that sets it against the ethical realm, as having nothing to do with ethics or with human responsibility, only responsibility to the new thing that is coming into being. ("Expecting" 36)

For Stephen Watson, *The Master of Petersburg* is performative, "dramatised through another of Coetzee's minutely realised theatres of cruelty . . . a meditation . . . of the diabolism that can lie at the heart of the creative process itself" ("The Writer and the Devil" 49) and a "drama of sin from which there is, apparently, no release" (60). Nowhere is such performative thought as prevalent, and nowhere is Dostoevsky's boundless imagination as evident as in the dialogic debate about revolution that takes place between Dostoevsky and Nechaev at the center of the narrative, a debate enacted by characters in costume, centered around the fable of the dog as potential sign.

When Dostoevsky first encounters Nechaev, the young revolutionary is in drag, dressed as a "heavily powdered" (100) woman, a "handsome creature" (100) for whom Dostoevsky feels "a flutter of desire" (98). Both characters, Dostoevsky and Nechaev, wanted by the law for vastly different reasons, must negotiate the city of St. Petersburg incognito. While the novelist gives up his charade as Pavel's father early in the narrative, a disguise that does not require him to occupy a subjectivity other than the one with which he is familiar, Nechaev continually embodies the subjectivity of a woman. He claims, "men dog your footsteps whispering such filth as you cannot imagine, and you are helpless against it!" (102). Through his performance of femininity—a performance good enough to fool Dostoevsky—Nechaev is able to empathize with the women who walk alone along the streets of St. Petersburg. Dostoevsky, on the other hand, is destabilized by his realization that the woman before him is a man, and such destabilization forces him to call into question the trustworthiness of external signification. He even begins to doubt that the Finn, Katri, is a woman. Femininity is rendered as "clownish" parody (156), and by virtue of this performance Dostoevsky is further alienated from being able to empathize with a feminine other, in the form of "real" women—like his wife, Anya, or Anna Sergeyevna, or Matryona—or of a man—like Pavel, Nechaev implies—who may be effeminate or homosexual (100, 160).[13] While the third-person narrator claims that Dostoevsky's imagination has no bounds, his reaction to Nechaev's enactment of femininity reveals that he is unable, no matter how hard he tries, to "resurrect" (52) or imagine the interiority of his stepson.

However, before he realizes that "the tall young woman . . . with the piercing blue eyes" (96) is in fact Nechaev, he restates the parable of the dog to Katri (while Nechaev is present) as he questions Katri about the relationship of revolutionary murder to the soul:

> Don't you become like someone called in from the street, a beggar, for instance, offered fifty kopeks to dispose of an old blind dog, who takes the rope and ties the noose and strokes the dog to calm it . . . and as he does so feels a current of feeling begin to flow, so that from that instant onward he and the dog are no longer strangers, and what should have been a mere job of work has turned into the blackest betrayal . . . ? Wouldn't it deter you . . . ? (99)

Such questions evoke Dostoevsky's earlier decision to abandon the dog tied in the cold based on his belief that the dog is not the sign for which he is waiting. But the analogy between the dog and Nechaev's victims also asks that the revolutionaries identify with the subjectivity of the dog: "and if a mere dog can do that, what power will the men and women you propose to get rid of have to haunt you?" (99). Ultimately, Dostoevsky finds himself closely aligned to the revolutionaries he claims not to understand; as he begins to write *The Devils* at the end of Coetzee's novel, he realizes that "he has betrayed everyone; nor does he see that his betrayals could go deeper" (250). Such an assertion seems an indictment of the sympathetic imagination, the sensibility Dostoevsky evokes in his second telling of the fable of the dog. The artist's responsibility, it appears, is synonymous with the responsibility of the revolutionary: what matters is the creation itself, whether artistic or political, and not the means by which one creates.

As Stephen Watson asserts, "the sufferings that a novel like this records are . . . the sufferings of human beings who consider themselves souls" ("The Writer and the Devil" 59). Searching for signs leaves Dostoevsky empty handed, a soul in search of a connection with a dead son who will not speak from beyond the grave. Writing, however, creates signs, and it is through the act of writing that Dostoevsky engages with the death of his son, an engagement that I contend does not end in a "final impasse, a knowledge of damnation beyond the reach of any form of forgiveness" (60) as Stephen Watson claims. Instead, it is through writing that Dostoevsky negotiates and potentially disrupts the boundary between life and death, just as Coetzee negotiates the boundary between biography and fiction in his portrayal of the historical Dostoevsky (and something he does through the third-person narration in his autobiographical works *Boyhood* and *Youth*). In this sense, what must be recognized is the writing, and in a very literal sense the dog—especially in this novel—is Coetzee's written word, the sign within the text that is rendered literal entity when it is recognized by Dostoevsky. Despite his inaction when it comes to saving the dog, Dostoevsky is at least finally capable of the realization that the distinction between thing and sign is negligible, and he is perhaps closer to a recognition that one's humanity lies in one's ability to respond to the other regardless of the symbolic or self-serving power of such action. Otherwise, death will remain the only equalizer, the only moment when black and white, human and animal, achieve the same level of Kafkan wretchedness, living and dying, as Joseph K claims in *The Trial*, "like a dog" (231).

* * *

There is a sole black and white photograph situated on the page between Jillian Edelstein's forward and Michael Ignatieff's introduction to *Truth and Lies: Stories from the Truth and Reconciliation Commission in South Africa*. The photo depicts a high wall over which peer twenty black faces. All we can see of the people behind the wall are their heads and their hands, hands that grasp the top of the cinderblock division and pull the body upward. Below them is a small doghouse backed up against the wall and a chain running off from the wall to somewhere outside of the picture, beyond our frame of reference. Perhaps a dog is chained just outside of our view, or perhaps there is no dog anymore. Perhaps aligning black faces with the empty dog house is a visual metaphor for the treatment of black South Africans during apartheid, human beings who were, according to Ignatieff, "shot like dogs and burned like animals" (19) by people whose actions were confessed between 1995 and 2001 during the Truth and Reconciliation Commission (TRC), South Africa's attempt to set the record straight and tell the truth about what happened during apartheid. Despite the fact that the TRC succeeded on one level in that it "rendered some lies about the past impossible to repeat," according to Ignatieff, "South Africa remains what it is: a society where a person's chances in life are still determined by the colour of their skin" (20). The TRC marked the end of an era that began long before the National Party proclaimed apartheid in 1948, and the dog that is absent from Edelstein's photo may very well be the historical apartheid era watch dog that, like the dogs of the Nazi regime, served the white South African police state, instilling terror in black South Africans through literal attacks, or it may be the dog that protected whites against their own scapegoat, the projected fear of black South African intrusion. Or the dog may be the beloved, pampered, and sentimentalized white South African pet, an animal that often received more care and better food than the black masses relegated to the metaphorical doghouse of township life.

Perhaps, then, it is best that the dog is absent form Edelstein's photo, for who in South Africa can love the dog now, and how many of the people peering over the wall would like to kill the dog, to shoot it as do the rapists in Coetzee's *Disgrace*, to enact vengeance upon the dog and all it represents? Perhaps, if we try hard enough, we can imagine that the dog has been liberated or has escaped the injustice of life at the end of the chain. But Ignatieff is not writing about dogs or about animals at all when he writes about a group of people, black South Africans, who have historically been treated like dogs. The mentality that distinguishes between us and them—not between blacks and whites but between animals and humans—is not something that the Truth and Reconciliation Commission seems to have disrupted. Coetzee's writing, however, puts the dog back in the picture, so to speak, by granting the dog its alterity in a place that exposes the fallacy of confessional truth by bringing to the forefront resistance, a silence that will not be broken. Coetzee's writing is filled with dogs, both metaphorical and real, and the dog is what really matters, the primal and essential "other," the locus for all human potential reciprocity, and ultimately as itself, a being deserving of recognition, of care, and perhaps, primarily, of acknowledgement.

Chapter Three

Displacing the Voice:
Coetzee's Female Narrators

I thought talking and not talking made the difference between sanity and insanity. Insane people were the ones who couldn't explain themselves. There were many crazy girls and women. (Maxine Hong Kingston, *The Woman Warrior* 186)

Who is speaking me? (Susan Barton, J. M. Coetzee's *Foe* 133)

As I stated in the previous chapter, in a colonial or capitalist framework, women and animals serve the same symbolic function, but the connection between women and animals, according to Lori Gruen, "is not to be understood as a 'natural' connection—one that suggests that women and animals are essentially similar—but rather a constructed connection" (61). By recognizing this "constructed connection," the ecofeminist argument espoused by critics like Gruen is careful to avoid the essentializing rhetoric that equates women with nature and men with culture while still recognizing the ways that othering animals is a preliminary cognitive step towards othering humans, a step that is further complicated by variables like gender and race. If, as Elizabeth Fisher claims, "the keeping of animals would seem to have set a model for the enslavement of humans" (197), as I have argued in my previous chapter, the animal in a metaphorical literary sense serves as a silent stand-in for enslaved or oppressed human beings like the indigenous South African men and women depicted in novels like Coetzee's *Dusklands*. Coetzee furthers the constructed connection between animals and women in *Waiting for the Barbarians* when the Magistrate equates the silent barbarian girl with the fox that he keeps in his rooms, but in *Disgrace*, the animal signifies for itself, functioning as neither metaphor for black South Africans nor for white women when it is positioned between women like Lucy and Bev and the black men who invade Lucy's farm. Coetzee can write the animal body into his narratives because the animal is a body devoid of spoken language, a body that must signify for itself as a body. Women, on the other hand, speak, and Coetzee's voicing of women via his female narrators, Magda in *In the Heart of the Country* (1977), Susan Barton in *Foe* (1986), and Elizabeth Curren in *Age of Iron* (1990), raises questions of narrative authenticity and the ethics of speaking this specific other.

Just as the dog shifts from simile to symbol to signified in Coetzee's corpus, his female narrators shift from allegorical entity to metaphorical character to Coetzean persona, and while Coetzee's three female narrators do not necessarily constitute a continuum despite the fact that they follow one another chronologically in his oeuvre and in this study, they are illustrative of a progression in Coetzee's ability to express an identification with the feminine and, in the case of Elizabeth Curren, perform femininity within his narratives. This aspect of feminine performativity becomes most fully realized and most fully fused with Coetzee's representations of the animal body in his 1997–98 Princeton Tanner Lectures entitled *The Lives of Animals,* a work written as two fictional lectures—therefore two lectures within two lectures—delivered by the fictional novelist Elizabeth Costello. *The Lives of Animals* was published first as a distinct text in 1999 and then subsequently as "lessons" three and four of the eight lessons that comprise the first novel to be released after Coetzee won the Nobel Prize, *Elizabeth Costello* (2003). I will examine that particular work more closely in the final chapter of this study, but here I will foreground my discussion of the character of Elizabeth Costello with a critique of the female narrators that contribute to Coetzee's later performance of a feminine subject position in *The Lives of Animals.* In terms of their progressive nature, Susan Barton and Elizabeth Curren build on and enrich our understandings of several concepts introduced initially by Magda in *In the Heart of the Country:* the seeming impossibility of writing the female subject position into history without constant entrapment by a self-negating narrative; the difficulty of occupying any clearly defined role during a colonial, apartheid, and/or gendered interregnum; and the perhaps unworkable desire to connect with the other, either in human or animal form. That Coetzee chooses to address such issues from the perspective of white female narrators is illustrative of his own tendency to identify with the position of white women as both complicit with and victimized by patriarchal and colonial institutions like those of apartheid and literary production.

Students of literature are constantly instructed to recognize the distinction between the author and narrator of a text; the narrator's voice and position are not necessarily the voice and position of the author, and to make such an assertion constitutes a naive theoretical faux pas at best. But many scholars seem to question the disjunction between the narrative and authorial voice when it comes to Coetzee's female narrators, perhaps because voicing the feminine seems such an overtly political strategy from an author who constantly refuses to be political, or perhaps because we think that Coetzee's politics are closely aligned with those expressed by the female characters he voices. In fact, of Coetzee's third female narrator Elizabeth Curren, Derek Attridge seemingly conflates the authorial and narrative positions, asking, "does it make sense to ask which?" ("Trusting" 64) when discussing Curren/Coetzee. The discomfort of identification that these narrators create among Coetzee's readers rests upon a disquieting fact: given what we do know about Coetzee, it is safe to assume that he feels a certain and understandable degree of unease with his masculine subject position, complicated as it is by his status as white in South Africa. How closely identified could he possibly want to feel, and truly, how closely can we align him, with his male narrators like Jacobus Coetzee or Eugene Dawn in *Dusklands,* or even the more sympathetic Magistrate in *Waiting for the Barbarians?* Being white and male in South Africa is to inhabit the subject position of colonizer and apartheid beneficiary, a position with which Coetzee is clearly at odds. As I have previously stated, even his autobiographical pieces *Boyhood* and *Youth* are narrated in the third-person, a device that serves to alienate the author from a self he reluctantly claims as his own while disrupting our notion of authorial and narratorial verisimilitude in the realm of autobiography.

When Coetzee chooses to narrate via a first-person narrator, that narrator is more often than not female, not because Coetzee is usurping a voice, but because he genuinely identifies with the white female subject position in South Africa. As Sue Kossew claims,

> the voice of the white woman coloniser is the ideal vehicle [for Coetzee] . . . encapsulating as it does the ambivalence of the non-existent middle ground, in a situation where only "yes" and "no" are heard. It could also be argued that this is exactly the position in which any "liberal" white writer has found her/himself in apartheid South Africa. ("Women's Words" 23)

The female voice is the voice from which Coetzee speaks something as close to the truth as possible, if there is any such thing as truth to speak, and raises questions about the very concept of confessional truth-telling. The divide between truth and lie is negligible in these narratives that seem foregrounded in the contradictory notion that all narratives are both true and false and, therefore, that no narrative is either true or false. This idea is clearly illustrated through the confessions of these female voices from Magda's contradictory assertion that "I have uttered my own life in my own voice" (139) despite her earlier claim that "what I say does not come from me" (7), and Susan's assertion that "I will not have lies told" (40) despite her complicity in the lie that she is Mrs. Cruso, to Elizabeth Curren's ultimate claim that "there is no lie that does not have at its core some truth" (187). Because it attempts to signify a narrative middle ground, the white female voice is the voice that is at liberty to be the most self-consciously critical of peoples and politics in a colonial milieu, yet it is a voice that is granted only a modicum of authority. And it is this voice from which Coetzee questions all concepts of ownership, including ownership of the narrative. As beings that are both owned and owning, Magda, Susan, and Elizabeth ask who owns who? Who owns the land? And who, if anyone, owns the story?

In her now famous essay, "Can the Subaltern Speak?," Gayatri Chakravorty Spivak claims "if, in the context of colonial production, the subaltern has no history and cannot speak, the subaltern female is even more deeply in shadow" (83). Spivak's essay is, of course, required reading for any critic who wants to discuss the intersections of postcolonialism and feminism, and it perhaps stands at the forefront of a movement of feminist differentiation in its placing of the subaltern female subject in a category distinct from her Western sisters, just as Alice Walker's term "womanist" sought to differentiate between white feminist rhetoric and black women's sociopolitical concerns in the United States in the 1970s. It seems wise, therefore, to foreground any discussion of Coetzee's female narrators as feminist (or antifeminist) with some brief contextualization of the postcolonial feminist debate, almost all of which, at least in its codified and canonized current format, quite tellingly, has very little to say about South Africa. According to Chandra Talpade Mohanty, to ascribe an all-encompassing and Western feminist category of "woman"

> to women in the third world colonizes and appropriates the pluralities of the simultaneous location of different groups of women in social class and ethnic frameworks; in doing so, it ultimately robs them of their historical and political agency. (213)

Sara Suleri furthers this assertion when she says that "the coupling of postcolonial with woman . . . almost inevitably leads to the simplifications that underlie unthinking celebrations of oppression, elevating the racially female voice into a metaphor for 'the good'" (246), the female "noble savage" of imperialist imagination.

By and large, the feminist critics who theorize issues of race, ethnicity, and womanhood in terms of the postcolonial speak from and for a non-white female subject position; such a stance is characterized by colonialism's double bind of race and gender as they compound to influence constructions of third world women. In terms of the South African situation, this same double bind certainly exists for indigenous South African women. But what are the feminist concerns of white South African women who, instead of finding themselves caught within two systems of patriarchal oppression, find themselves in-between, stranded on literal and figurative islands as both colonial dominators (white) and subjected, second-class citizens (women)? I would argue that these two conflicting tensions serve, if not to effectively cancel each other out, to create a tension around the act of testimony that serves to silence a white South African feminist agenda—and Coetzee's female narrators, Magda, Susan, and Elizabeth, through the presentation of their continually self-negating narratives, serve to illustrate such a position.

In fact, attention to the concerns of both black and white women in South Africa have been by and large pushed to the background because, according to M. J. Daymond, "the issue of power has been focused on race and has seldom been gendered in South African writing;" therefore, "black and white women now face major obstacles to the development of a community of purpose" (xix). The fact that the first feminist session at the annual conference of the Association of University English Teachers of Southern Africa took place in 1980 (Lockett 3) points to the relative lateness with which South African women joined a visible and international academic feminist debate. The situation is easy to understand given much more visibly pervasive issues of racial politics in South Africa, politics explicitly addressed by South Africa's most prominent white female author, Nadine Gordimer, an author who, as I stated earlier, has historically been wary of the moniker of "feminist." In more recent years, however, such a stance has provoked current South African feminist critics to decry Gordimer's "ambivalence, even quixoticism" (Lazar 283) with regard to the plight of South African women. It is worth noting that Gordimer's work is critiqued in this way primarily because she is a woman and is therefore expected to write about issues that affect her country's women. In her avoidance of an explicitly expressed feminist agenda, Gordimer's stance is akin to Coetzee's in its refusal to write explicitly political narratives of South Africa. Both authors, regardless of their personal stances for or against various representations that speak to a specific political agenda, do, however, address both issues of race and gender in their works.

While Coetzee reluctantly voices non-white others, a choice Michael Marais claims is illustrative of "respect for their alterity" ("Little Enough" 164), through his white female narrators, he will voice white women. In Coetzee's work, women, like animals, shift from voiceless subjects/signs in his male-narrated texts (for example, the barbarian girl in *Waiting for the Barbarians*) to articulate presences (like Elizabeth Curren in *Age of Iron*) in his female-narrated novels. Coetzee's project can be read as an attempt to resurrect a feminine ethos repressed by patriarchal colonial politics; in fact, the trinity of Magda/Susan/Elizabeth constitutes the archetypal matriarchal triad of virgin/mother/crone. Coetzee's female narrators in *In the Heart of the Country, Foe,* and *Age of Iron* attempt to fulfill the role of mediator often occupied by white women as both colonized and colonizing. Also, as the voice of the reluctant colonizer, Coetzee identifies with his female narrators; according to Sue Kossew, "his white women narrators . . . are represented as ambiguous colonial figures whose voices are compromised by complicity, a complicity from which his own authorship is never excluded" ("Women's Words" 12). In terms of Coetzee's ethics, the white female voice may be one of the only authentic places from which to speak: for Coetzee, the use of the feminine narrative voice represents the disjunction between his self-proclaimed denial of the paternal—of having two mothers and no father in *Boyhood*—and his socially ascribed position as white, South African, and male.

Such claims are very contentious: Coetzee has been criticized by feminist critics who believe, as Kirsten Holst Peterson does, that his feminine narrative voice is "an assertion of appropriating male authorship" (qtd. in Kossew, "Women's Words" 13) and an inauthentic attempt at ventriloquism. Similarly, Josephine Dodd, who regards South African literature in general as "a pretty sexist affair" (327), claims that in *Foe,* "as fast as Coetzee exposes the colonial intent . . . he reenacts it himself" (331). To complicate matters, his female narrators, Magda and Susan Barton, for example, have traditionally been read, rather reductively, as allegorical (Collingwood-Whittick, DuPlessis, and Briault-Manus). Just as Coetzee has been accused of avoiding "the apartheid question," it is equally easy to read his writing as antithetical to a true feminist thrust, evasive as it is of "the woman question." But South African feminism is nascent, in the midst of its own interregnum, and the issues of gender-based injustice as distinct from and interconnected with issues of racial oppression are still seeking postmodern voices to speak them. According to Pamela Ryan,

The conservative forces of the establishment . . . insist on providing labels for those groups of people which they wish to marginalize; how then can a "feminist" retain a commitment to the cause of feminism on the one hand and to the "reality" of the political situation of South Africa on the other? A related problem is equally relevant: when postmodernism denies the possibility of the coherent individual self, how is it possible . . . to write about the "real" historical female subject in South Africa? (31)

Perhaps Coetzee, "strictly observant of feminist rules," as Regina Janes claims, and "the first deliberately female-identified writer our tradition has produced" (107), has found at least one productive way to deal with this dilemma: writing women under the auspice of fiction, Coetzee exposes the fallacious reasoning that there can be any consistent notion of the "real." His narration from a fictitious female perspective, therefore, in its conscious execution, brings to light the very impossibility of voicing the "real," historical, female subject that Ryan discusses. The notion that there is ever a representable "real" is too closely aligned with the idea of the circular and contradictory "truth" of confession—an act, according to Coetzee, of "a regression to infinity of self-awareness and self-doubt" ("Confession" 274)—for Coetzee's comfort.

THE CONFESSIONAL VIRGIN: MAGDA AND *IN THE HEART OF THE COUNTRY*

Magda . . . may be mad . . . , but I, behind her, am merely passionate.
(J. M. Coetzee, interview with David Attwell, *Doubling the Point* 61)

Coetzee's first female narrator, the white, Afrikaner Magda in *In the Heart of the Country* (1977) describes herself as "an absence" (2) and "a spinster with a locked diary" (3). Throughout the novel, she references the intersection of her status as regrettably sexually innocent with her status as violently, patricidally experienced; she is the "miserable black virgin" (5), "jagged virgin" (8), and "fierce mantis virgin" (116) who, in various numbered narratives, repeatedly murders her father. Magda immediately tells the reader that her narrative is not to be trusted, quite frankly because she does not exist, is a fiction like the narrative she relates or translates, someone to whom the reader cannot ascribe agency. Second, as a virgin whose latent sexuality creates a pattern of circular destruction—of the narrative, of the father, and of any form of human intimacy—Magda is a kind of self-proclaimed cipher that desires to be the "medium," "neither master nor slave, neither parent nor child, but the bridge between" (133), but fails for reasons directly attributable to her race and gender. Finally, her voice is not her own; it belongs to someone else, perhaps to Coetzee as an exercise in narrative production, perhaps to history as the narrative of white female desire that continuously cancels itself out in the treacherous imperial outpost of the rural South African landscape depicted—without direct reference to a specific time period—in *In the Heart of the Country.* Over the course of the novel, Magda speaks or writes multiple and numbered narratives that shift, alter, and negate the veracity of her previous narratives. At one point, Magda kills her father and his new wife with an axe, but then the narrative voice turns speculative as she states *"perhaps* I strike out once or twice with wooden arms" (13, my emphasis). She cleans up the blood and disposes of the bodies only to claim shortly thereafter, "he does not die so easily after all" (16) as her father rides off into the sunset. Later in the narrative, Magda kills her father again after he has a forced affair with his servant Hendrik's wife Anna, only to have him crop up, "a mannikin of dry bones held together by cobwebs" somewhere inside of which "juices still dribble" (136–7) at the end of the novel.

Dominic Head points out that in many ways *In the Heart of the Country* is "Coetzee's most difficult and forbidding novel" (*J. M. Coetzee* 49), and Ian Glenn claims that the novel is the "least read and has had the least critical attention" (120) in part because of its difficulty. With regard to Magda, several questions demand immediate attention: is she a character or is she an allegorical manifestation as many critics have claimed? Is this novel an allusion to Schreiner's *Story of an African Farm,* or does the constant reappearance of Magda's dead father echo the recurrent black dead body in Gordimer's *The Conservationist*? Does Coetzee usurp a female voice when he writes via Magda, or does Magda function, as Glenn claims, as Coetzee's *"alter ego* who can explore the dilemmas of the colonial writer cut off from the landscape and its inhabitants" (128)? And in any case and perhaps most importantly, why does Coetzee choose to narrate this particular story (or these particular numbered narratives) from the perspective of a woman—a question that, in my opinion, has never been adequately answered by the various voices of critical commentary. Magda's narrative is a narrative of desire, the specific desire of a white woman for language, for sex, for connection, and for salvation, within a context that repeatedly negates those desires. Dominic Head claims that as an allegorical phenomenon and literary subject, Magda is an "anomaly because she finds herself in a literary genre (pastoral) to which her passion does not belong" (*J. M. Coetzee* 66); furthermore, of all of Coetzee's female narrators, Magda most fully represents the way that the white female voice continually negates its narrative as it attempts to take up a position in a system not of its own making (colonial and/or apartheid South Africa), but a system within which it is nonetheless privileged and complicit. If that voice attempts, as Magda's does, to confess its way out of such a paradigm, claiming "I am not simply one of the whites, I am *I*!" (118), it also turns back on itself, appropriating the voice of the white patriarch she repeatedly and unsuccessfully attempts to kill. For example, she uses racialized language when she screams at Hendrik, "you damned hotnot, it's all your fault" (91) after he refuses to help her bury her father's body.

According to Sheila Collingwood-Whittick, in *In the Heart of the Country,* Coetzee creates a work of metafiction and presents a narrator who "far from striving to convince the reader of the authenticity of the experiences she describes, contrives instead to cast doubt on the veracity of her narrative" ("Writing by Numbers" 16). If Magda makes no claims of authenticity, then Coetzee cannot possibly be usurping an authentic female voice, but his narrative strategy is nonetheless fraught with critical controversy. DuPlessis claims that Magda functions as a stereotype and that Coetzee's text fails to deal with "'women's experience' as it is understood by Anglo-American feminists" (119). Furthermore, he claims that readers should not

> attribute the presence of femininity in a text by a male author like Coetzee to some empathetic involvement in the condition of women. . . . The documentation or reconstruction of women's historical experiences takes place in a different arena, that of autobiography and testimony. (119)

Given, however, that Coetzee feels that "the self cannot tell the truth to itself and come to rest without the possibility of self-deception" ("Confession" 291), and given what we know about his feelings with regard to confessional narrative and autobiography—that the first is never trustworthy and the second is always, in some way, a product of the first—it stands to reason that the narrative voices that speak the "truth" in these genres described by DuPlessis are less reliable than the voice of Magda that is at least honest about its dishonesty and at least illustrates its own fallaciousness, a voice that tries out every possibility and option. With very few exceptions, critics do not read Magda as an actual character; instead, they argue, as Vicki Briault-Manus does, that she is allegorical, a figurative presence whose narrative is Coetzee's art, "endlessly opening up new possibilities of interpretation, and [whose] quest for identity is a test of the signifying power of language" ("*In the Heart*" 64). Conversely, Sue Kossew does read Magda as a character and claims that her desire to find an authentic language "is not just the desire for 'a woman's sentence' [in Virginia Woolf's sense] which would subvert the patriarchal structure but is also a desire to communicate on a level of equality with the 'downcast' colonised Others" ("Women's Words" 14). These various readings—metafictional, realistic, and feminist—point to the seeming impenetrability of this, the least studied of Coetzee's texts.

Magda's voice is an attempt for Coetzee to imagine the ways that a white South African woman of a certain time period—a period that comprises at least a century—might attempt to write the body, in Hélène Cixous's sense, to claim the body—"your body is yours, take it"—and to give up writing that is not good "because it was in secret, and because you punished yourself for writing, because you didn't go all the way" (Cixous 335), writing that would appear, for example, in Magda's locked diary (3). *In the Heart of the Country* is, if not directly informed by Coetzee's familiarity with the French feminists like Cixous and Irigaray who were writing during the early and mid-1970s, at least informed by the ethos to which their writing responds. Cixous calls out for women to write, to overturn the "imbecilic capitalist machinery" that oppresses, but she also notes that "woman must write woman. And man, man" (335). Magda's voice, therefore, is a game played by Coetzee: an aggressive unvoicing, an impossibility in Cixous's sense, the woman written by a man. Furthermore, she is a woman who tries to write her way out of this negation, to constantly confess her crimes of murder and solitude, to rewrite the narrative until she can claim, "I have chosen every moment of my own destiny" (139). But because of Magda's placement in this particular South African context and because she ascribes to the Freudian sentiment that designates her an absence, an emptiness, "around which lingers in horror, now and forever, an overcathexis of the eye, of appropriation by the gaze" (Irigaray 405), her story is also an absence. If we read the variations of the rape of Magda, for example, and choose to believe the first which involves Hendrik's "beating" and "kicking" (104) of her, then we cannot also believe the fifth telling in which Hendrik gently seduces Magda, telling her, "don't be afraid" (107). Essentially, we cannot believe any of these options, or we must believe them all simultaneously. Magda becomes the symbolic manifestation of white female desire in South Africa, ignored and self-negating, complicit with and critical of apartheid, a motherless daughter in a political framework that would prefer her to be a son.

Despite the fact that Glenn somewhat reductively dismisses the conspicuous absence of Magda's mother "less as a limiting condition on Magda . . . than as a way of avoiding complications to the plot" (134), the absence of the mother highlights the presence of the father and the overdetermination of the patriarchal in this novel and in a colonial framework in general. As Magda says, "my father is the absence of my mother. . . . He has murdered all that is motherly in me and left me this brittle, hairy shell with peas of dead words rattling in it" (37). In *In the Heart of the Country*, the position of the narrator whose words rattle endlessly in circuitous cancellations must be female and furthermore emblematic of womanhood without a literal and figurative female model. In many ways, Magda's voice is the white, feminist South African voice seeking recognition, a recognition it has only newly begun to attain. Furthermore, were Magda not female, her status as virgin/spinster would fail to signify as synonymous with the interregnum South African landscape, and while such a comparison can be read as essentializing, it also serves to underscore the palpable absence of female agency and power throughout South Africa's colonial history. Magda's "love of nature, particularly of insect life" (6) fuses the connection between her body and the land, both of which are dry and hard.

The land and its inhabitants are infertile at this historical juncture; Magda cannot reproduce—cannot even be forced to reproduce by Hendrik—just as in *The Story of an African Farm*, Lyndall cannot replicate the present because the present is becoming obsolete. Magda can imagine a kind of virgin birth, the product of which would be "the Antichrist of the desert" (10), but when she kills her father and his new wife, death itself is depicted as the only reproduction of which Magda may be capable as she attends over and over to the "bloody afterbirth" (15) of these murders. Through Magda, Coetzee unwrites the archetypal virgin whose destiny is to reproduce, perpetuate, and deify the masculine. As a parody of the Christian duality of Virgin Mary and Mary Magdalene (for whom she may be named), the quintessential virgin and whore, Magda subverts the notion of Immaculate Conception and the salvation that it supposedly engenders. If Magda is allegorical, then she represents woman as a linguistic phenomenon or Coetzee's attempted expression of a white, South African female position and its subsequent silences. But Magda is silent before she even begins, claiming, "what I say does not come from me"(7), admitting to the reader that what she says comes from the realm of male interpretation and the male gaze, her father's disappointment that she is not a son and Coetzee's self-aware inability to write woman as anything other than woman imagined by man.

THE CANNIBALIZED MOTHER: SUSAN BARTON IN *FOE*

As for fictional confession, this mode is already practiced by Defoe in the made-up confessions of sinners like Moll Flanders and Roxana; by our time, confessional fictions have come to constitute a subgenre of the novel in which problems of truth-telling and self-recognition, deception and self-deception come to the forefront. (J. M. Coetzee, "Confession and Double Thoughts," *Doubling the Point* 252)

If Magda provides a critique of confession in that she is aware that what she says does not come from her, Susan Barton in *Foe* (1986) is "doubt itself" (133), less certain of who controls the truth of her narrative. Unlike Magda who tells her own story, an elaborate exercise in continual negation of that narrative, Susan's story of her life as a castaway on Cruso's island is taken from her by Foe, Coetzee's fictional representation of Daniel Defoe, who wants to write the fabricated story of Susan's reunion with her long lost daughter. While Magda is a spinster without a mother, Susan is a mother whose only daughter is abducted two years prior to the narrative only to reappear as Foe's creation—"father-born" (91)—a girl Susan claims is not her child but is a girl conjured or hired by Foe: "do you think women drop children and forget them as snakes lay eggs?" (75), she asks the child. Despite the fact that Susan searches for her daughter in Bahia, she eventually abandons hope and embarks for Lisbon on the ill-fated voyage that brings her to the island of the reticent Cruso and face to face with the voiceless Friday. At the center of this narrative, as in *In the Heart of the Country*, is the woman's desire to tell a story, in this case, the story Cruso does not care to record and that Friday cannot tell because his tongue has been cut out, according to Cruso, by slavers who are also cannibals and perhaps "hold the tongue to be a delicacy" (23). After she is rescued, Susan chooses to tell her story to Foe, the "author who had heard many confessions" (48), and Foe's insistence upon creating a narrative of maternal reunion in spite of Susan's denunciation of a narrative that "traduces [her] account" (Attwell, *J. M. Coetzee* 110) essentially revises her character in order to assert patriarchal control over her story, experience, and sexuality. The narrative that restores the child to the mother is less subversive than Susan's indecent narrative of a woman who abandons the search for her daughter only to wash ashore on an island inhabited by two men, one of whom is black and the other with whom she engages in a sexual relationship outside of wedlock. And despite Susan's assertion that "I will not have any lies told" (40), she participates in the charade, claiming that she is Mrs. Cruso for the sake of her reputation. As a white woman, Susan's narrative is already compromised by virtue of her concern with proper gender-based appearances and by her complicity with certain aspects of the revision/cannibalization of her identity at the hands of Foe and the masculinized historical narrative he not only writes but that his character in Coetzee's novel also represents.

Women have had a difficult time of writing themselves into history, no matter how well they may been received by the public during the time they were writing. For example, in 1719, novelist Eliza Haywood sold nearly as many copies of *Love in Excess* as Daniel Defoe sold of *Robinson Crusoe* (Backscheider and Richetti x), but Haywood's body of work—and from 1719 to 1756 she wrote over 60 novels in which her heroines disguise themselves and subsequently displace gender norms (Schofield 24)—has only begun to receive any scholarly attention. Magda and Susan effectively serve to illustrate the plight of writers like Haywood and, more importantly, of women whose stories never make it to the page. These narrators share certain commonalties, just as Coetzee's female-narrated texts share certain characteristics. Both women desire to tell a story, and both are castaways, who like Dostoevsky in *The Master of Petersburg*, seek external signs to support and buffer their internal narratives. Susan interprets the rocking of the island as "a sign I'm becoming an island dweller" (26) while Magda claims she is "spoken to not in words . . . but in signs" (7) and wonders if she should "imitate the classic castaways and light a pyre to draw [the] attention" (131) of the airplanes that fly overhead.

For both women, as for most of the women that populate Coetzee's fiction, their first sexual encounters in the contexts of the narratives are, if not definitively rape, forced interactions for which the narrators make excuses. When Hendrik rapes Magda, she retells the encounter numerous times perhaps to make it more palatable to herself, transforming it from violence to seduction. Similarly, when Cruso ignores Susan's initial rebuff of his sexual advances, she excuses him by telling her audience and herself that "he has not known a woman for fifteen years, why should he not have his desire?" (30). Such instances highlight the nature of these white women as the complicit victims of male domination and of violence that is enacted not only on their bodies, but also on the bodies of their black counterparts, on the bodies of animals, and on the land itself. By excusing such sexual violations, these narrators maintain a complicity that enables their violators to perpetuate the more pervasive violence of colonization, violence often foregrounded on an explicit presentation of the animal/human dichotomy. For example, while Susan sees "no harm" (21) in the apes that inhabit the island, in a move that foreshadows Elizabeth Costello's later complicit decision in *The Lives of Animals* to carry a leather handbag despite her militant vegetarianism, Susan wears ape skin sandals just as she is willing to masquerade as Mrs. Cruso to save her reputation.

As in *In the Heart of the Country*, *Foe* again raises questions of narrative authenticity: if the historical Defoe is a fiction in Coetzee's text, how are we to gage Coetzee's own reality, his own ability to relay the truth through fiction, a truth that he borrows or appropriates from other authors? According to David Attwell, Coetzee alludes to three novels in *Foe:*

> Susan Barton's narrative replicates this feminist self-affirmation [of Lyndall in Schreiner's *Story of an African Farm*], specifically by taking the island conditions of *Robinson Crusoe* and overlaying them with the narrative of Defoe's *Roxana*, whose picaresque feminine hero's real name is, of course, Susan. (*J. M. Coetzee* 106)

Sue Kossew defends Coetzee's appropriation of Defoe's narratives by claiming that one reason for "Coetzee's choosing to 'write back' to Defoe is seen to relate to Defoe's tendency to exploit women's stories, so that many parallels are drawn between Susan and both Moll Flanders and Roxana" ("Women's Words" 17), and M. Gaye et al are in agreement with Kossew when they claim that "the introduction of female gender into the Crusoean world [a world that they claim is highly homoerotic] signals a provocative departure from a literary heritage and Coetzee's intention to settle accounts with Daniel Defoe" (132). In this sense, one can read Coetzee's project as feminist revisionism, a critique of the male appropriation of women's writing presented through Coetzee's appropriation of Defoe's "master narrative," a narrative, in Coetzee's telling, that "belongs" to Susan Barton.

But such a reading is problematic for two reasons. First, if we consider that Coetzee without attribution also borrows from Adrienne Rich's *Diving into the Wreck* (as various feminist critics like Josephine Dodd and Regina Janes have claimed), Coetzee can be accused of enacting the very appropriation his text critiques. Conversely, however, there seems to be no debate about the ethics of Coetzee's referencing Schreiner's *The Story of an African Farm*, quite possibly because critics allow Coetzee to allude to this most instrumental South African text without direct attribution. The problem with the Rich critique, therefore, stems from a matter of definition: when is an author plundering the work of another—specifically when the author in question is male and the work is written by a woman—and when is he merely alluding to that work in a way that is artistically and academically acceptable or even in a way that pays homage to that work? And furthermore, if part of Coetzee's point is to illustrate that no one owns the story, then the question of direct or indirect reference becomes utterly meaningless. Secondly, Susan's feminist impulse to tell her story is perhaps negated by her inability to ascribe human status to Friday claiming that she gives "to Friday's life as little thought as [she] would have a dog's or any other dumb beast's—

less indeed" (32). However, Susan refers to herself as an animal as well, claiming that her voice is as meaningless as a magpie's when she speaks to Friday. For Barbara Hall, such references are evidence of "the processes of dehumanization, the method so efficiently mastered in colonization and its consequences" (22), but they may also point to a need for the acceptance of the other as other, without a prerequisite explanation. Again, the animal reference functions to represent the body devoid of language, unable to ask for or give anything, expecting nothing that it can vocalize, yet still worthy of respect.

At its core, *Foe* is a narrative of the explicit vampirization of the white woman's story and body by male appropriating forces—Cruso, Foe, and (perhaps self-critically) Coetzee—and of the fictitious cannibal upon which this literal vampirization is projected, in most cases, Friday or someone racially like him. Cannibalism as a trope is very often explicitly present in Coetzee's opus, from Jacobus's paranoid descriptions of cannibals to his own cannibalistic enactment when he bites off an African child's ear in *Dusklands*, to Magda's assertion that she is a mantis—the insect that devours its mate—in *In the Heart of the Country.* The act of writing is also conceived of as implicitly cannibalistic in Coetzee's work by critics like Janes who claim that in *The Master of Petersburg,* "the father . . . rewrites the dead son . . . eating him up" (112). In *Cannibalism and the Colonial World,* edited by Francis Barker, Peter Hulme, and Margaret Iversen, the authors claim that while cannibalism may have existed historically, in the colonial ethos cannibalism functions as a myth, a linguistic phenomenon signifying the ultimate power of capitalism, projected by colonizers onto colonized peoples in order to other and justify the colonial impulse to "civilize the savages." According to Hulme, cannibalism "marked the world beyond European knowledge . . . ready to reappear when civilisational influence showed signs of waning" (3). In this sense, the figure of the cannibal is merely a "screen for colonial violence" (9). While Hulme acknowledges the fact that both sides of the colonial equation believed tales of human consumption—"in the nineteenth century . . . the fear of cannibalism ran both ways, with Africans often convinced that whites were buying them in order to eat them" (35)—his focus is on disproving such stories and showing instead their rhetorical power in the service of the colonial enterprise.

Unseen cannibals pervade *Foe* and, according to Cruso, inhabit the island, but Susan is reluctant to believe in their existence, and it is her ability *not* to believe in this projected justification for colonization that places Susan at best outside, or at the least, on the boundary of the colonial position. Of Friday, Cruso tells conflicting stories in which sometimes Friday is a former slave, "at other times," Susan claims, "he would tell stories of cannibals, of how Friday was a cannibal whom he had saved from being roasted and devoured by fellow cannibals" (12). Furthermore, according to Cruso, cannibals inhabit Brazil and Africa, but Susan is suspicious and wonders whether Cruso cut out Friday's tongue (84) thereby enacting colonial domination and cannibalizing Friday's story, controlling his narrative and telling one version and then another, neither of which she is able to fully trust. Similarly, later in a scene that places her in the same subjected position as Friday, Foe tells Susan, "I would not rob you of your tongue for anything" (150) by stealing her story. When they are kissing, however, Foe conflates Susan's narrative and her body, and gives her "such a sharp bite to [her] lip that [she] cried out and drew away. But he held [her] close and [she] felt him suck the wound" (139). Foe becomes Cruso's elusive cannibal who devours the woman's story, robbing her of her narrative voice and her ability to write herself into history, providing her instead with an "acceptable" and destabilizing narrative, the return of her absent daughter. She says to Foe

> In the beginning I thought I would tell you the story of the island and, being done with that, return to my former life. But now all my life grows to be a story. . . . I thought I was myself and this girl a creature . . . speaking words you made up for her. But now I am full of doubt. . . . Who is speaking me? (133)

Coetzee further undermines the reader's ability to determine who is speaking whom in part four of the novel, when the narrative voice shifts from Susan to two unknown narrators, both of whom enter Susan's story to find Cruso, the captain, and Foe indistinguishable from one another and, like Susan, dead. The only character whose body is still warm is Friday, and the narrator(s) presses "a fingernail between the upper and lower rows" (154) of his teeth, "trying to find a way in" (157) to the black hole of his mouth. Ultimately, it is Friday's wordless story, "the sounds of the island" (154) and the "slow stream, without breath, without interruption" (157) that emerges and devours the other narratives by displacing Susan/Coetzee's quests for meaning, signifying instead in a place where "bodies are their own signs" (157). After all of the other storytellers in the novel are dead, their "skin, dry as paper . . . stretched over their bones" (153) or their bodies "fat as pigs . . . puckered from long emersion" (157) underwater, Friday's body alone lives to haunt the text, asking to be read in its own right.

THE ACADEMIC CRONE: ELIZABETH CURREN IN *AGE OF IRON*

> Elizabeth Curren brings to bear against history and historical judgement that resound around her two kinds of authority: the authority of

the dying and the authority of the classics. (J. M. Coetzee, interview
with David Attwell, *Doubling the Point* 250)

At the end of *Age of Iron* (1990), when several boys try to pry narrator Elizabeth Curren's teeth apart as she lies feverish beneath an overpass, they are not
in search of her story but want instead the gold in her teeth. While Friday's
voice remains unheard in *Foe,* Elizabeth Curren's narrative position as former
classical literature professor is obsolete during the apocalyptic interregnum of
Coetzee's fictionalized Cape Town of 1986. By the time Coetzee wrote *Age of
Iron* in 1990, the distance between narrator and author was becoming less
easily definable, and Derek Attridge feels compelled to assert this distinction
when he claims that the letter Elizabeth Curren writes to her daughter "is J.
M. Coetzee's as well as Mrs. Curren's gift (even though we must keep distinct
the operation of posthumous letter and published fiction)" ("Trusting" 61).
Unlike the more metafictional Magda and the cannibalized, metaphorical
Susan, Coetzee's third female narrator, the elderly, terminally ill Elizabeth
Curren, is a fully formed character who embodies the epistolary text she
writes to her daughter overseas. Also unlike her previous incarnations, Elizabeth is willing to relinquish control of her narrative in an act of uncondi-
tional trust. Like Magda, Elizabeth is Afrikaner, and like Susan, she is a
mother who has lost her daughter, in this case, to the enticements of the
United States, leaving Elizabeth symbolically barren and forever seeking an
elusive and viable maternal role, aware that "we embrace our children . . . to
pass ourselves on beyond death" (5). Like Coetzee, she is a South African
academic, and her expertise as a classical scholar has been displaced by the
nascent mythology of the interregnum of social and political upheaval
depicted in the novel.

   While in many ways Elizabeth Curren prefigures the displaced academic David Lurie in *Disgrace,* she also constitutes another aspect of Magda
and Susan; like them she is mateless, seeking comfort from a man who will
not tell her his story, seeking to tell her own story to herself and those who
come after her, matrilineal words for her daughter to "devour or discard" (9).
The elderly aspect of this female trinity, "a crone of death" (143), she thinks
of her cancer as a cannibalistic pregnancy, "children inside me eating more
everyday" (64). For Elizabeth Curren, the maternal is absent in South Africa,
and she must find a way to reconstitute it in her old age, to work against the
"death-driven male constructions" (150) that she feels are behind the violence in her country. Of the South African land she claims that once she
would have said, "*this is my mother,*" but now she no longer loves the land,
claiming, "I am like a man who has been castrated" (121). Her reproductive

barrenness parallels the barrenness of the land, and Elizabeth claims that "for twenty years I have not bled" (64); her cancer is her metaphorical pregnancy, the only thing that her body can create under such historical circumstances. Her illness with its rampantly increasing cells becomes a kind of deadly fetus, the product of the Afrikaner agenda for which a cure is unlikely but for which she may atone through the writing of the letter to her daughter. In *Age of Iron* as in *Foe,* Coetzee again undertakes the rewriting of another canonical and male-authored work of literature, this time the *Aeneid.* In Coetzee's revision, Elizabeth Curren, along with her housekeeper Florence and Florence's cousin Mr. Thabane, takes an apocalyptic journey to the metaphorical underworld of South Africa's black townships after which she is finally able to claim a kind of maternal responsibility for the body of the unlovable, black, township boy, John.

Along with the influence of the *Aeneid,* Coetzee's narrative was also inspired by personal hardships, the deaths of both of his parents and the death of his son, Nicolas (Huggan 191). In this particular narrative and through the voice of Elizabeth Curren, Coetzee carefully inscribes himself into a more agreed upon version of history. According to Sheila Collingwood-Whittick,

> as one who, by birth and racial identity . . . belongs to a society that is in the shadow of last things, Coetzee . . . gives free reign in *Age of Iron* to his own need to pursue certain important truths both about himself as a white South African and about the culture within which, despite his strong moral condemnation of it, he has the indissoluble link of historical complicity. ("In the Shadow" 45)

For Coetzee, this period of interregnum was not only marked by personal loss, but by profound social upheaval and "violence of cataclysmic proportions, the death of thousands of blacks in the cities and townships of the embattled Republic" (Huggan 191). Elizabeth is initially only marginally aware of her position as oppressor, and Coetzee places her in the epic role of Aeneas—a mythical character who has no practical application in 1980s South Africa—in order to reappropriate that particular narrative. Through interactions with the more marginalized members of South African society with whom she has immediate and intimate contact, the family of her black housekeeper Florence, Elizabeth attempts to find her way out of "the interregnum between a decaying, old political order and a new one seeking to establish itself" (Marais, "Places of Pigs" 87). Elizabeth's journey in *Age of Iron* constitutes an apocalyptic parable that ends with an enigmatic embrace from which "no warmth was to be had" (198), but her ability to embrace the homeless and surly Vercueil despite the fact that he makes no promises to her is potentially hopeful, the first step toward a kind of altruistic responsibility for the other. Coetzee's choice of Book Six of the *Aeneid* as source of intertextual subversion is significant because, according to R. D. Williams, it is in the later part of this book "that Virgil comes nearest to a solution of the problem of human suffering with which the whole poem is so preoccupied" (191). In Book Six, the Cumaean Sibyl takes Aeneas into the underworld in search of his father. While Aeneas seeks and confronts the paternal in the form of his father Anchises, Coetzee's Elizabeth Curren seeks the maternal and finds it in Florence (whose daughters, Hope and Beauty, function as abstractions, never materializing except rhetorically within the narrative) and finally in her own ability to care for Florence's son Bheki and his comrade John.

When Elizabeth Curren, who is in many ways the stereotypical elderly and solitary caretaker of cats, learns from her doctor that she has terminal cancer, the news causes two simultaneous occurrences. First, Elizabeth takes in a homeless man, Mr. Vercueil, and his dog who have been sleeping in a shack made of cardboard and plastic in an alley beside her garage, and second, she begins to write a letter largely about Vercueil to her daughter who has left South Africa for the United States refusing to return unless the situation improves. Tellingly, Elizabeth connects with Vercueil through the dog and claims that she trusts him because of the dog; according to Elizabeth, dogs are able to "sniff out what is good, what evil;" they are "patrollers of the boundaries: sentries" (84–5). In typical Coetzean fashion, the dog becomes the basis for Elizabeth's ability to comprehend the alterity of the other: "in the look that [Vercueil] gives me I see myself in a way that can be written. . . . When I write about his dog I write about myself" (9). Vercueil's arrival corresponds with Elizabeth's acceptance of her terminal status, and he becomes her silent and at times disdainful companion, the messenger to whom she entrusts, despite his ambivalence, the delivery of the letter after her death. The care she takes of Vercueil and his dog is a care independent of the promise of any sort of reciprocation, but it is nonetheless care given because it is seemingly expected from Vercueil. Conversely, when John is hit by a police van, Elizabeth is left alone with him to staunch his bleeding before the ambulance arrives, but she confronts Florence asking why she must be responsible for John and stating, unequivocally, "he is nothing to me" (65). To claim responsibility for John, who Elizabeth compares to a sick and feral cat she once nursed and that treated her as "the enemy" (79), is the more difficult and essentially necessary task than caring for Vercueil.

Elizabeth's housekeeper, Florence, functions as the sibyl when she returns to Elizabeth's home with her children in order to escape the violence of the township in which the black family lives, and it is Florence and other women like her who must ultimately occupy the maternal position and voice a new agenda after the interregnum has passed. Bheki and his friend John are committed to the political struggle for liberation in South Africa, and despite the fact that she is willing to admit the reticent and disdainful Vercueil into her home, Elizabeth is initially reluctant to recognize the black South Africans as members of her family; when John comes to stay with Bheki, Elizabeth says to Florence, "I cannot turn my home into a haven for all the children who run away from the townships" (54). Elizabeth is perhaps more accepting of Vercueil because, according to Derek Attridge, he is "a man so removed from the structures of social and political life that he even appears to have escaped the grid of racial classifications on which apartheid rests" ("Trusting" 62). But Vercueil can only take her part of the way; he is the messenger and ferryman, and, as Graham Huggan claims, "neither ferryman nor passenger can cross the threshold" (203). The classical mythology that once provided Elizabeth Curren with answers in the form of literary references—she tells John that if he had been in her Thucydides class, he "might have learned something of what can happen to our humanity in time of war" (80)—does not allow her access to a different mythology that exists in John's township home of Guguletu, a place that is beyond her realm of comprehension.

In *Age of Iron,* as in his preceding female-narrated texts, Coetzee again provides a critique of authorial and historical truth. Graham Huggan claims that Elizabeth Curren, as a former classics teacher, is a "ventriloquist of the dead" (196); furthermore, she ventriloquizes a particular dead tradition, that of white men: the stories told in classical texts, even the stories of goddesses, do not fit into the South African context within which Elizabeth finds herself in the late 1980s. By the same logic, Coetzee becomes the ventriloquist for the dead Elizabeth Curren. Since Vercueil will (perhaps) deliver her letter after her death, Coetzee's novel constitutes a kind of fictitious, posthumous document. Elizabeth says, "because I cannot trust Vercueil I must trust him" (130), and the fact that Coetzee's novel exists may be a testament to that trust: after all, must Vercueil have sent the letter, despite his ambivalence about doing so, for us to be able to read Coetzee's novel? But when Elizabeth tells John her own narrative, the story of her life, it is as meaningless as the classics she ventriloquizes. Elizabeth is, however, at least able to realize the meaninglessness of her words and to accept their status as trebly negligible because they are "the words of a woman . . . of an old woman . . . but above all of a white" (79). Elizabeth's ability to recognize her position within this metaphorical Iron Age is her saving grace; according to David Attwell, "Mrs. Curren is capable not only of refusing to see the other as non-human, but also of reading herself *through* those she is disinclined to love" (*J. M. Coetzee* 170). The position she self-consciously occupies is that of a white, "the color of limbo" (92), who ultimately is able to give, to her daughter, to Vercueil, and finally to John, without reciprocation.

Elizabeth offers to drive her housekeeper to the township after Florence learns of Bheki's participation in revolutionary violence, and there they find Bheki's body along with the bodies of four other boys in a burned-out school building. Elizabeth is shaken, and this apocalyptic moment allows her the opportunity for transformation. According to David Attwell, "South Africa means not only death . . . but also . . . an engagement with history that is in itself an act of transcendence" (*J. M. Coetzee* 125). Elizabeth's engagement with this violent historical moment is transcendental; she must find her way home alone, unaccompanied by Florence and rebuffed by Mr. Thabane who tells her to follow the "signs to civilization" (107). But despite the absence of her guide, Elizabeth is able to apply a new mythological interpretation to her dream about her housekeeper; she does more than merely ventriloquize its narrative in the dead terminology of classical literature. Of the dream, Elizabeth claims that Florence is an incarnation of a classical yet simultaneously new Aphrodite and realizes that "forever the goddess is passing, forever caught in a posture of surprise and regret, I do not follow" (178). Elizabeth can go as far as to conjure the goddess in the form of her housekeeper, but she is aware that she can go no further: the maternal future for South Africa is for the black woman and her children to define and perform.

Because she realizes that the interpretation of her written and translated version of the truth is obsolete, Elizabeth thinks seriously about setting herself on fire, thereby turning her body into a sign, but she realizes that the significance of the act may be as easily misinterpreted—as an act written on her body, it may be as easily misread—as the letter she writes to her daughter: "an old woman sets herself on fire," she says to Vercueil, "why? Because she is driven mad? Because she is in despair? Because she has cancer?" (114). Ultimately, Elizabeth Curren is able to relinquish the narrative of her writing and her body when she entrusts both her letter and body to Vercueil, allowing him to do with both what he will, just as she is able to relinquish her role as a ventriloquist when she recites for Vercueil "Virgil on the unquiet dead." When Vercueil asks for a translation, Elizabeth says, "it means that if you don't mail the letter . . . I will have a hundred years of misery" (192). Of course this translation is a fabrication; the passage is the sibyl's explanation to Aeneas that Charon the ferryman only transports the souls of the buried.

The unburied, Charon claims, must wander for a hundred years before they may go with the ferryman (Virgil 154). This passage directly relates to Elizabeth's earlier narrative about the spirits of the murdered, unburied boys in the township: she believes that "their ghosts have not departed . . . and will not depart" (104). Elizabeth's invented translation of the Latin language, like Coetzee's reinscription of the *Aeneid* itself, indicates a realization that these modes of discourse are obsolete in the interregnum, and Elizabeth must translate a "new truth," a truth that is in the process of being written.

When police shoot and kill John at the end of the novel, Elizabeth speaks in his defense and goes to ambulance that holds his body, claiming, "I want to go with him" (157). She has moved from a belief that he has nothing to do with her to the knowledge that she is responsible for him—or at least responsible for his dead body, for being his guide after his death—just as she is responsible for Vercueil and his dog, and just as neither Florence or Mr. Thabane owe any measure of responsibility to her. At the end of the novel, Elizabeth approaches Mr. Vercueil as he stands looking down at a "sea of shadows" (198), the symbolic River Styx beneath the window. When she climbs into bed, Mr. Vercueil takes her in his arms and holds her in an embrace that forces the breath from her lungs and may, in fact, end her life. Coetzee, through Elizabeth, indicts the dead language of the *Aeneid* just as he indicts the racist and patriarchal politics that have repressed the maternal and the black in South Africa. When she asks the spirit of her mother to come to her, Elizabeth claims that "she would not. Stretching out her arms as a coasting hawk does, my mother began to ascend into the sky" (55). Before Elizabeth can transcend, she must descend into the underworld with Florence, the goddess/sibyl whose maternal example, that of black, township mother, Elizabeth, as an Afrikaner, is unable to follow and that Coetzee is unwilling to voice. Florence and her family provide the only hope for the future, and Elizabeth, as a white woman, is no longer able to act as a sign for the maternal, but her realization of that fact is promising. The future stalks forward, and we must wait through the interregnum in order to see what form the goddess will take.

Chapter Four

Resisting the Voice: Waiting for the Magistrate and Michael K

This world divided into compartments, this world cut in two is inhabited by two different species. The originality of the colonial context is that economic reality, inequality, and the immense difference of ways of life never come to mask the human realities.

* * *

At times this Manicheism goes to its logical conclusion and dehumanizes the native, or to speak plainly, it turns him into an animal. (Frantz Fanon, *The Wretched of the Earth* 39 and 42)

When asked to comment on Tony Morphet's reading of *Foe's* Friday as a character who resists the reader's efforts to glean his interior meaning, Coetzee responded by saying, "I hope that a certain spirit of resistance is ingrained in my books; ultimately I hope they have the strength to resist whatever readings I impose on them on occasions like the present one" (Morphet 464). Clearly Coetzee's answer pointedly resists Morphet's question—just as Friday resists Morphet's interpretation—by refusing to grant the interrogator insight into the interior meaning of the character, text, and author. Ironically, by virtue of his own unreadability, Coetzee aligns himself with Morphet's interpretation of a resistant Friday, and with his own act of resistance, seemingly makes Morphet's case for him. In this sense, resistance becomes a kind of engagement with the interrogator, silence a kind of admission: we learn more from both Friday and Coetzee's refusals than we might from a more confessional answer. A chief difference between author and character, however, seems to be that Coetzee's refusal is active while Friday's is the result of the loss of his tongue at the hands of some unknown assailant. Such a characteristic perhaps makes him not only unwilling to tell his story, but physically and mentally unable.

Unlike Friday, the characters of Michael K and the Magistrate actively refuse, as Coetzee does, to tell their stories to audiences who seek confessions from them. The character of Michael K in *Life & Times of Michael K* (1983) more actively practices silence as he withholds his narrative from people who want him to open his heart "and tell them a story of a life lived in cages," the life of an animal, "a budgie or a white mouse or a monkey" (181). Similarly, the silence of the Magistrate, the first-person narrator in *Waiting for the Barbarians* (1980), is a refusal to confess to Colonel Joll the details of his journey to return a barbarian girl to "her people," and as a result, he is tortured and "kept alive perhaps only as evidence of the animal that sulks in every barbarian-lover" (124). The struggle of the two characters that I discuss in this chapter is the struggle to somehow escape from the various camps—and camp mentalities—that pervade the Fanonian concept of a colonial "world divided into compartments" (39) where one must always be at war, positioned on one side or other of a literal or metaphorical fence.

By relentlessly questioning his complicity within a regime that engages in the bodily torture of its colonial subjects, the Magistrate seeks escape through the intellectualization of his ambivalent position as a champion of an anachronistic imperialism. The Magistrate attempts this escape through a denial of the bodily manifest in his repeated washing of the tortured body of the barbarian girl. Michael K, on the other hand, is the colonial subject who attempts to escape *through* the body. More specifically, through starvation, he seeks to remove his body from the equation of war and from individuals like the medical officer—who is very much like the Magistrate in his attempts to care for and understand the narrative of trauma that marks Michael's body—who require him to provide them with a confession of his suffering as a way of intellectualizing and therefore justifying their own positions of ambivalence. But in the "not yet" space of the interregnum that marks both narratives, neither character is able to signify as anything other than a rhetorically constructed animal by the powers from which they seek to escape. They are held, against their wills, within a framework that, at the moment of the narrative action, will not allow for either character to exist outside of the binary structures that designate acts of refusal as subversive, dangerous, and deeply suspicious.

Reading *Waiting for the Barbarians* and *Life & Times of Michael K* in relation to one another allows for a critical mapping of the outside space sought by both characters, the space "out of all the camps" (182) for Michael, the space "outside of history" (154) for the Magistrate. Such a space, however, is an impossibility according to Michael Hardt and Antonio Negri in a chapter entitled "Imperial Sovereignty" in *Empire*—a chapter that begins with an epigram from *Waiting for the Barbarians* and ends with a close reading of *Life & Times of Michael K*:

> There is a long tradition of modern critique dedicated to denouncing the dualisms of modernity. The standpoint of that critical tradition, however, is situated in the paradigmatic place of modernity itself, both "inside" and "outside," at the threshold or the point of crisis. What has changed in the passage to the imperial world, however, is that this border place no longer exists. (182)

If "in the passage from modern to postmodern and from imperialism to Empire there is progressively less distinction between inside and outside" (Hardt and Negri 187), then such arbitrary distinctions as "inside" and "outside" must be constructed in opposition to some internal phenomenon. I contend that within the context of both *Waiting for the Barbarians* and *Life & Times of Michael K,* such a space can only exist in opposition to the physical pain inflicted on the bodies of both characters and can therefore only exist internally; no outside is available to either the Magistrate or Michael unless it is *within* the realm of the imaginary, the only space from which one can experience an alternate reality devoid of pain and suffering.

In *The Body in Pain,* Elaine Scarry links this imaginary space to trauma inflicted on the body: "pain and the imagination are each other's missing intentional counterparts" (169) in that

> imagining is, in effect, the ground of last resort. That is, should it happen that the world fails to provide an object, the imagination is there . . . as a last resort for the generation of objects. Missing, they will be made up; and though they may sometimes be inferior to naturally occurring objects, they will always be superior to naturally occurring objectlessness. If no food is present, imagining grain or berries will, at least temporarily, allow the hunger to be experienced as potentially positive instead of wholly aversive; and the imagined image may remind the person to walk over the next hill to find real wheat and berries. (166)

Ironically, then, in both works the literal outside space that these characters seek as a form of last resort is symbolically available, at least for the present interregnum moment, only through the imagination. Both the Magistrate and Michael do imagine alternate realities in response to physical suffering, specifically the abuse and starvation inflicted on the Magistrate by his torturers and self-inflicted by Michael, and both are ultimately able to imagine a reciprocal relationship with other human beings—even if those others are imaginary—a relationship that is impossible within the current war-determined context of both narratives. While the Magistrate wants to be fat again and actively seeks the food he has been denied—Scarry's theoretical grain and berries—imagining "a belly that gurgles with contentment when [he] fold[s his] palms over it," and wanting "to feel [his] chin sink into the cushion of [his] throat . . . never to know hunger again" (130), he is initially unable to imagine the barbarian girl or the torture she has suffered. He thinks, "if I took a pencil to sketch her face I would not know where to start. Is she truly so featureless?" (47). While Michael, on the other hand, makes no attempt to imagine sustaining his body by providing it with food at the present moment, at the end of the narrative he is able to imagine not only a future in which sustenance might be possible, but a future in which he is guided by another human, an imaginary "old man" who "knew the roads" (183). Later in *Waiting for the Barbarians,* after he has been tortured, the Magistrate is able to dream that the barbarian girl smiles at him, and he can envision all of her features, her eyes, her hair, her "beautiful teeth" (109), even if those features do not correspond to her real appearance. Despite his efforts to capture these images by writing "the truth" (154) of his experiences, he is unable to record his experiences—real or imaginary—by the end of the novel.

The concept of "the truth" in both works is dependent upon an understanding of the connection between writing, torture, and the realm of the imaginary as these variables function to establish the designations of insider and outsider. In *Imagined Communities,* Benedict Anderson credits the printed text in the form of the novel and the newspaper as "two forms of imagining" (25) that serve to construct the imagined community of the nation; the daily newspaper became a collectively practiced prayer-like ritual that provided selective access to the rest of the world, and the novel allowed readers to experience the simultaneous occurrence of multiple events within a paradigm that conflated space and time in order to present concurrent narratives. Adam Smith identifies imagined access to the sensations of others in the context of socially sanctioned punishment: "Though our brother is upon the rack, as long as we ourselves are at our ease, our senses will never inform us of what he suffers. . . . It is the impressions of our own senses only, not those of his, which our imaginations copy" (qtd.

in Bender 220). In the context of Smith's analysis, imagined sensory identification allows individuals of more fortunate circumstances, those of us "at our ease," to empathize with those who are less fortunate, "our brother[s] on the rack." In turn, according to Moses, "most distressingly, Coetzee renders writing (inscription and interpretation) as a form of torture" (120) in that in both novels, the act of writing inscribes outsider status, and functions, like torture, to rob the subject of access to the interior truth of the self.

In *Waiting for the Barbarians,* Colonel Joll writes the word "ENEMY" in the dust on the backs of his prisoners, and then soldiers beat the word from the flesh (105). The word alone justifies the removal of the word by violence; the prisoners become enemies because such status is written into being, in a language they cannot comprehend—English—and inscribed externally on a part of the body—the back—they cannot view. Any internal narrative that the "enemy" can offer becomes meaningless in the face of codification if the motive of torture, according to Elaine Scarry, is "the obsessive display of agency that permits one person's body to be translated into another person's voice, that allows real human pain to be translated into a regime's fiction of power" (qtd. in Wenzel 63). In a more benevolent codification that mirrors the ideology of the Magistrate while it simultaneously points to the fiction of confession by virtue of writing or torture, the medical officer in *Life & Times of Michael K* encourages another officer named Noël to write a fabricated account of Michael's experience for the official report. When Noël objects, the officer says, "it's not a lie. . . . There is probably more truth in the story I told you than you would ever get out of Michaels if you used thumbscrews on him" (141). Either Michael's or the medical officer's narrative, therefore, would be equally suspect, and the officer's fictitious report, while it benefits Michael (at the expense of those it may implicate), is written under the assumption that Michael is a "poor idiot" who is "not of our world" (142). Furthermore, the medical officer, by virtue of the fact that he refers to Michael as "Michaels," has already inscribed for Michael an alternate and fictional identity through his own misreading of the protagonist's name. Rhetorically constructed as a barbarian, Michael is classified and codified through writing, like the prisoners in the Magistrate's experience, by words written behind his back.

* * *

Most critics have tended to read the Magistrate in *Waiting for the Barbarians* rather reductively as a character who is too caught up within his current conceptual framework to be able to fully understand his role within it, or as

Michael Valdez Moses reads him as "an inverted version of Conrad's Kurtz" who is "both the enlightened hope at which his civilization aimed and its failure to fulfill those hopes" (119). Wendy Harding's claim that "even though he seems acutely self-conscious and deeply reflective, the narrator is finally too committed to inherent modes of thought to be able to imagine an existence apart from the one he already knows" (215) and Dana Ringuette's belief that the Magistrate "finally has no overarching, generalized knowledge of his situation, apparently—nothing more than the very local, immediate awareness of his own circumstances" (9) must be read with some skepticism. First, both Harding's and Ringuette's readings ascribe to the narrative a finality that is inappropriate to the open-endedness of the Magistrate's closing sentiment that he is a man who "presses on along a road that may lead nowhere" (156). Second, the "inherent modes of thought" to which the Magistrate is committed are modes of thought that nonetheless preclude government-sanctioned torture: his resistance to and defiance of Joll's regime point to a desire to imagine an alternate framework, even if that regime is still implicated in the workings of Empire, and even if other possibilities cannot be imagined at the present time. Lindan Lin reads the Magistrate as a character whose compassion "suggests that racial prejudice and hatred are not universal conditions and that they can be subverted by people of the privileged class" (53). While such a reading is hopeful, it also tends a bit toward the utopian; within his current position, the Magistrate may try to subvert specific conditions, but his attempts are largely unsuccessful. Furthermore, Lin's claim that the sexual relationship between the Magistrate and the girl is "mutually fulfilling" (53) fails to acknowledge the power dynamic that drives their sexual interaction: the Magistrate, despite his beneficence, is the servant of Empire while the girl's continued existence depends entirely on Empire's whim—and neither the Magistrate nor the girl seems particularly fulfilled by the sporadic and complicated sexual interaction that results from their relationship.

In *Waiting for the Barbarians,* the Magistrate, a long-time servant in a fictitious imperial outpost, is initially a believer in the greater good of the colonial project. He nonetheless resists the overt cruelty of torture, a means of extracting the "truth" introduced by the new, sunglasses-wearing face of the Third Bureau of the Civil Guard, Colonel Joll. Despite the Magistrate's assertion that "there is nothing to link me to torturers, people who sit waiting like beetles in dark cellars" (44), he is guilty of an insidiously oppressive paternalism in the form of what he assumes to be benevolent colonialism. While the Magistrate initially believes himself to be the antithesis of the cruel Colonel Joll—a distinction he recognizes only after

Joll's regime performs acts of torture in close proximity to him—he comes to realize that their goal is essentially the same, to gain access to the "truth" through the body of the other. In the Magistrate's mind, his actions are distinct from those of Joll, but he comes to see similarities between the way both men "hunt back and forth, seeking entry" into the narrative and the body of the girl and wonders, "is this how her torturers felt hunting their secret, whatever they thought it was?" (43). While he seeks a way into the narrative of the girl's tortured body—a narrative to which she is unable or unwilling to grant him access—through a kind of nurturing care, he behaves "in some ways like a lover," but the Magistrate alternately recognizes, "I might equally well tie her to a chair and beat her, it would be no less intimate" (43). After Joll leaves, the soap and water the Magistrate demands in order to make "everything as it was before" (24) illustrate a desire to move back through history to an imaginary time "before" the torture took place, but he is unable to create such a past and realizes that his cleansing rituals constitute instead an attempt to forget. He admits, "I begin to face the truth of what I am trying to do: to obliterate the girl" (47) and later claims, "I am forgetting her, and forgetting her, I know, deliberately" (86). This attempt at obliteration is a willful refusal to see the girl if she does not grant him access to her narrative of torture, and washing in *Waiting for the Barbarians*, like hunger in *Life & Times of Michael K*, becomes an act of counterproductive purification, an attempt at resistance that ultimately fails to succeed.

The fact that the Magistrate is able to recognize certain similarities between himself and Joll ironically also saves him from being like Joll; because he seeks another mode of signification, we cannot make a one-to-one correlation between the Magistrate's actions and those of Joll. Furthermore, the Magistrate's desire to gain entry into the girl's narrative is predicated upon the fact that she has been tortured. Therefore, his insistence upon her confession does not arise from, as it does in Joll's case, the desire to inflict pain.[1] The Magistrate continually recognizes and critiques the fact that he, like Joll, is guilty of the paternalistic impulse he views with disdain, and, despite his persistence and apparent benevolence, the girl denies him access to a "confession:" a litany of unthinkable acts of torture committed on her body, acts he cannot imagine. According to Ali Behdad, "dissolution can be achieved either through a cold-blooded militarism—discipline, torture, and pain—or through a benevolence and humanism that embodies pleasure, desire, sexuality" (203), and the Magistrate's narrative focuses on such benevolence as he nurses, washes, has sex with, and cares for the barbarian girl after she has been blinded by her torturers. According to Jennifer Wenzel, "just as there is no answer the girl could give to satisfy Joll's need for the 'truth,' there is no story the girl could tell that would make the Magistrate certain of her pain" (66). Similarly, the Magistrate later denies Joll access to his own confession and is physically punished for this refusal. While we never see the torture chamber that contains the girl and, like the Magistrate, never have access to what is done to her, the Magistrate does graphically describe his own beatings and privations, thereby enacting the very confession he seeks from the "other;" through his telling of the circumstances of his own suffering, the Magistrate ultimately is able if not to actively imagine, at least to passively dream about what the girl might have been like prior to her torture. The act of telling the story of his own torture—or Coetzee's act of writing that story—links the act of confession to the Magistrate's ability to engage with the sympathetic imagination.

Furthermore, while the Magistrate views the girl as "other," as a woman whose "femininity is associated with darkness and animality" (Harding 212), his ability to analyze his identification with Joll indicates that he is also in possession of a double consciousness that allows him to critique his own treatment of the girl as well. Ultimately, he decides to take her back to her people, despite the fact that they have dispersed as a result of Joll's attack, and he does so fully aware of the punishment he may incur upon returning to camp. Despite such beneficence, he is never able to fully understand or transcend his own motives for trying to decode the narrative of torture written on the girl's body. When he returns her to her home—or to his idea of her home, since no real home exists for her anymore—he claims, "I am with her not for whatever raptures she may promise or yield but for other reasons, which remain as obscure to me as ever" (64). This inability to see what motivates his actions is a kind of blindness that results in a failure of the sympathetic imagination, the Magistrate's inability to imagine the torture inflicted upon the body of the girl. According to Brian May, "the Magistrate can neither cast off the body nor exalt it, and his imaginative capacity scarcely comes across as a personal failing, connected as it is to his horror at what Empire is doing to bodies" (405). Even "his realization that the girl must be returned is a lesson learned through experience and error, a change in thought that comes unexpectedly not merely as a reaction to Joll but through his relation to the much different, 'alien' presence of the girl" (Ringuette 24). Such commentary is correct in that the Magistrate, someone who believes in "an archaic code of gentlemanly behaviour toward captured foes" (108), is initially unable to comprehend and therefore ultimately rejects his role in the torture of the girl, a leap that would require his mental identification with her. His inability to make this leap, however, is not a cognitive failure; the Magistrate does recognize his culpability and his implication in Joll's regime, but there simply exists, at the present moment, no external space in which he can behave—or even imagine behaving—differently.

At the level of torture, however, the Magistrate's body is forced to identify with the body of any suffering creature, including women, children, and animals, that ranks beneath him in the colonial, patriarchal hierarchy. For example, when he, like the girl, is blinded from a blow across his face, he initially identifies with insects—perhaps the beetles he compares to the torturers—and thinks, "it occurs to me that we crush insects beneath our feet, miracles of creation too" (107). Later in his cell, he identifies with children: "I finally give way and sob from the heart like a child" (109). In *Waiting for the Barbarians,* the penultimate result of torture, just prior to the production of a lifeless body, is to be reduced to an animal. After the barbarian girl is tortured, the Magistrate equates her with an animal and gives her a fox, saying, "people will say that I keep two wild animals in my rooms, a fox and a girl" (34). Later in the narrative, when he takes her back to "her people," the Magistrate again describes her as an animal, capable of speaking to other animals: "the girl stands with her arms outstretched like wings over the necks of two horses. She seems to be talking to them: though their eyeballs glare, they are still" (67). Despite his best intentions, such comparisons point to the Magistrate's continued belief in a system that designates women inferior to men and animals inferior to humans. But when the Magistrate is tortured, he is forced to occupy the rhetorical space of both woman and nonhuman creature; his torturers dress him in a woman's smock and hang him from a tree by his arms, "a foot above the ground like a great old moth with its wings pinched together, roaring, shouting" (121). The bodies of the fox, the girl, the horses, the moth, and the Magistrate signify simultaneously through their respective suffering: the body of the fox trapped inside the Magistrate's rooms and the bodies of overworked horses terrified of a storm differ hardly if at all from the body of the girl trapped in the camp, or the tortured body of the Magistrate lifted from the earth against its will. At this point in the narrative, after his torture, the Magistrate, who has been unable to imagine anything at all, is able to imagine the girl about whom he dreams with intense specificity: "her hair is braided in a heavy plait which lies over her shoulder: there is gold thread worked into the braid" (109).

But interestingly, one of the most profound ways that the Magistrate differs from Joll and his regime is in terms of his previous *inability* to imagine the existence of the enigmatic barbarians, to realize instead that the fantasy of barbarian invasion is an enabling colonial myth. The fear of the barbarians by the servants of Empire in *Waiting for the Barbarians* is projected by a regime capable of atrocities—the same fear caused by the vague and intangible threat implied by the possibility of a terrorist attack in the current socio-political context of the United States. In fact, in her essay, "Terrorists and Vampires: Fanon's Spectral Violence of Decolonization," Samira Kawash deconstructs Fanon's rhetoric of violence in order to examine the ways that in the 1980s and 1990s, "'terrorism' stands as [Fanon's] violence of decolonization gone global" (238). As a spectral presence always about to appear, the terrorist is like the vampire that threatens to destabilize the status quo of the imperial, phallocentric order. According to Kawash, the terrorist is "structurally similar to the ghosts and vampires of the Victorian imagination, exemplary figures of the Freudian uncanny" (239). The barbarians in Coetzee's narrative occupy this same space, and, for the men of Empire, the barbarian presents a threat to women, thereby justifying male military posturing and female subservience, a myth that the Magistrate clearly questions early in the narrative:

> There is no woman living along the frontier who has not dreamed of a dark barbarian hand coming from under the bed to grip her ankle, no man who has not frightened himself with visions of the barbarians carousing in his home . . . raping his daughters. These dreams are the consequence of too much ease. Show me a barbarian army and I will believe. (8)

In Coetzee's narrative, "barbarian," like "terrorist," becomes a floating signifier devoid of specific meaning. The Magistrate's continued denouncement of the myth of barbarian existence at the end of the novel—"we have no enemies . . . unless we are the enemy" (77)—functions to conflate the us-and-them dichotomy, the same dichotomy that constructs him as other from the girl and that allows him the potential for imagined identification with her through his own bodily suffering.

In the interregnum space depicted in *Waiting for the Barbarians,* writing, like torture, according to Michael Valdez Moses, "is necessarily implicated in and complicit with the worst excesses of Empire" (120). The Magistrate's proclaimed inability to write "a message as devious, as equivocal, as reprehensible" (*Waiting* 154) as the history he, as a servant of Empire, could tell, at least resists imperial control of history via the written word "in order to render permanence where there is only transience" (Ringuette 17). Furthermore, at the end of the novel, his burial of the indecipherable poplar slips he finds while excavating ruins in the desert testifies to the existence of the interregnum, an historical period that is not ready to receive whatever meaning the slips may hold, but it also testifies to his belief that the slips may also contain devious equivocation. Writing, he realizes, is not to be trusted. The Magistrate's burial of the slips constitutes another attempt, like his ritual cleansing of the barbarian girl's body, at erasure and obliteration; he creates a mass grave for ancient words that refuse to stay buried, like the mass grave the well-diggers find about which the Magistrate claims, "we must fill it in and start again" (148). This burial also constitutes the Magistrate's attempt to preserve for the future that which cannot be comprehended in the present.

At the end of the novel, the Magistrate claims to "leave . . . feeling stupid" (156), and his stupidity may be insurmountable given the colonial context in which he finds himself, but the act of leaving, whether from the literal manifestation of his dream—children playing in the snow—or from the outpost itself, is perhaps the beginning of another kind of resistance, a refusal to remain stationary, to remain asleep and dreaming, within the confines of the incomprehensible and untrustworthy narrative of imperial history. If at the end of the novel the Magistrate still lives in his familiar outpost, recovered from his torture and maintaining his service to the an earlier incarnation of the Civil Guard, he has at least stopped short of writing the story of the outpost and thereby resists or refuses—at least on some level—participation in a framework that determines "the fundamental distinction between civilization and barbarism is that between the lettered and the unlettered" (Moses 117). The act of not writing, in fact, indicates an open-endedness indicative of the Magistrate's ability to at least imagine a different future narrative.

* * *

The critical tendency when examining Michael K in *Life & Times of Michael K* is often to place him in the company of two other Coetzeean characters, Friday in *Foe* and the barbarian girl in *Waiting for the Barbarians;* in fact, Tony Morphet refers to these three characters as a kind of "family" (463). Furthermore, Michael Naumann claims that while these characters are technically adults, they are also aligned as "children of the earth" because of "their special relations to the (Earth)-Mother positive imago, their taste for farming, their opposition to the harsh and all-powerful protestant father and their very limited mastery of language" (36). The language over which they have limited mastery is English, and Naumann's association of this lack of mastery with childlike status is problematic in that it prioritizes English while it makes somewhat reductive assumptions about these characters' abilities to access language. The implication, therefore, is that silence may be an inherent phenomenon instead of—as it often functions in Coetzee's texts—a form of resistance. But there are marked differences between Michael K and his two "siblings," the most profound of which is the fact that both Friday and the barbarian girl primarily resist not by active refusal to provide access to their interior narratives to the interrogator, but by virtue of a physically traumatic experience that hinders their own emotional access to a coherent interior monologue.

Prior to the narrative that takes place in *Foe,* Friday's tongue is cut from his mouth by some unidentified violator, and before the Magistrate meets her, the barbarian girl is blinded and tortured by Colonel Joll's regime. For the victim of torture, according to Jennifer Wenzel, physical trauma creates a reality in which the "truth is negated along with the voice of an integrated self" (63). The self cannot tell the "truth," the story of its own trauma, to itself after it has been tortured, much less to anyone else. As Elaine Scarry claims, the infliction of pain through torture not only has "the ability to destroy language," but also obliterates the consciousness of the victim of torture: "pain begins by being 'not oneself' and ends by having eliminated all that is 'not itself'" (54). Through the free indirect discourse of the third-person narrative position, the character of Michael K, unlike either Friday or the barbarian girl, engages in an interior monologue despite his active resistance to engaging in dialogue with anyone else. Michael, like these other characters, is also physically marked, his speech complicated by a cleft lip, but Michael's trauma is inadvertent, the result of a birth defect and not externally imposed torture (though this marking may function as torture in terms of the way that it negatively affects Michael's life). Furthermore, the starvation Michael endures over the course of the narrative constitutes a specific act of refusal that results from his choice not to eat even in the face of the availability of food.

Other critics of *Life & Times of Michael K* have focused on the novel's environmental and ecocritical value and have examined Michael's position as a gardener who strives to produce food not for himself but for those who will come after the war has ended, and whose care of the land functions in service of the environment for the sake of the environment. Derek Wright claims that "Michael K is a hero for the white ecological Eighties" (440), even as he reads the character of Michael as black; such a reading is problematic given that Michael's race is never clearly identified within the narrative.[2] It seems more fitting to read Michael's failure to signify within any racial categorization as evidence of the medical officer's claim that Michael is "a great escape artist" (166), the variable that resists categorization. Mike Marais recognizes the connections between the land, the colonial subject, and an absent maternal as they are manifest in *Life & Times of Michael K,* claiming that "in Coetzee's fiction, the issue of negation is often tied to the subject's domination of nature" (108). Patricia Merivale reads Michael's starvation as an indictment of a political system that oppresses human beings by dominating the land: "Coetzee's politico-economic point is that Michael needs for his sustenance explicitly that food which he is free to grow for himself" (161). David Attwell reads the metafictional nature of Michael's character and claims that

> K remains his own person: in refusing to be imprisoned in any way, either in the literal camps or in the nets of meaning cast by those who follow after him, he becomes—in the socially symbolic field of the novel's engagement with South Africa, that is, in the field of reading and interpretation—a principle of limited, provisional freedom, a freedom located in the act of writing. (*J. M. Coetzee* 92)

Such a position seemingly negates Derek Wright's reading of Michael as a black man whose, "story cannot be written" (441) but can only by imagined by a white writer. For both Michael and the Magistrate, the story that can or cannot be written—depending on whose critical interpretation one accepts—is a story that explores the possibility of imagining a change in the existing structures of power that, nonetheless, remain in place for the duration of the narrative.

The body of Michael K, as a result of its emaciated androgyny, refuses to signify via familiar markers that denote masculinity and femininity as well as race and age (the medical officer in Part Two believes that Michael is older than his self-proclaimed thirty-two). His unreadable body allows Michael a subject position that straddles binary oppositions by representing at once a declining South African patriarchy and unformed or suppressed femininity. Through starvation, Michael is further able to identify with women, children, animals, and even insects, just as the Magistrate, through torture, is able to empathize with these entities. Michael thinks of himself as a mother, as "a woman whose children have left the house" (111), after he destroys his pumpkins to avoid detection by the army. He also claims that he comes "from a long line of children without end" (117), and later while living in a burrow in the ground, he returns as an unborn child to the womb of "mother earth" just as the anorexic woman, according to Kim Chernin, "regresses to infancy but does not get reborn" (175). While the Magistrate feels like a moth when he is hung from a tree, by the end of the novel, Michael believes that he is "more like an earthworm" (182), an unspeaking, unseeing insect, than a gardener. Speech furthers the disjunction between the mouth's primary function, eating, and its socially imposed task of communication. Michael speaks and eats only sporadically throughout the novel, and no other character in the novel is able to interpret Michael's speech after the death of his mother. In fact, misinterpretation marks Michael's speech as well as his silence, the text of starvation he inscribes on his body.

The third-person narrator of *Life & Times of Michael K* tells us that Michael K's adventure begins "in the thirty-first year of his life" (4) as he quits his job as a city gardener, picks up his mother from the hospital, and begins the journey that will take him and his mother, Anna K, away from Cape Town toward Prince Albert. Anna dies en route to the Visagie farm, her childhood homestead for which she has grown nostalgic, and while she is in the hospital, Michael dreams that his mother brings him "a parcel of food" (28) that becomes manifest in the parcel of his mother's cremated ashes that are later given to him by a nurse. Michael's mother is an ineffectual nurturer because of her poverty, but a reconnection with or creation of a fecund femininity is a desirable goal in the infertile landscape of a South Africa embroiled in the civil war that provides the backdrop for the narrative. For Michael, the land and the mother are intimately related and ultimately fused after he later mixes her ashes with the soil in which he grows the pumpkins that symbolically signify as his children. After receiving the parcel of his mother's ashes, Michael's first utterance is indicative of all of his enigmatic spoken discourse after his mother's death. He asks the nurse, "how do I know?" (32), but she does not understand his question, and he makes no attempt to explain his meaning.

The reaction of the other characters to Michael's ambiguous use of language is frustration and anger; language functions for Michael K as Michael K functions within the context of the narrative. In part two, the medical officer points to the allegorical nature of Michael K as an example of "how outrageously a meaning can take up residence in a system without becoming a term in it" (166). The character of Michael K, like the term "barbarian," becomes a floating signifier, present within the text but devoid of any fixed meaning. According to Luc Renders, Michael, like his use of language, is not "a representative figure who models certain forms of behavior or capacities for change; rather, he is an idea floated into a discursive environment that is unprepared to receive it" (100). This lack of preparation is the result of the period of interregnum, the "not yet quite," in which Michael and the other characters in the novel find themselves.

Despite his mother's death, Michael continues toward Prince Albert, and at this point in the narrative, he continues to eat. At first he buys food, but later he scoops mealies and bone meal from a feeding trough used by livestock animals, claiming "at last I am living off the land" (46). When he reaches what he believes to be the Visagie farm, he begins to tend the earth by turning over his mother's ashes in the soil and planting pumpkin seed. He resumes his role as gardener, no longer as an employee of the state, but as a cultivator of the earth for this earth itself. The act of cultivation for Michael K lays the literal and figurative groundwork from which may grow the options for an alternative South African future beyond the current moment characterized by Coetzee's fictional civil war. According to Derek Wright, Michael K "plants to keep the earth, not himself, alive . . . it is done, if for anyone, not for the present, but for posterity" (439) in the hope that by the time the food ripens, the war will be over. However, he leaves his plants to die when Visagie's grandson returns to the farm and assumes that Michael is the caretaker employed by his grandparents. Michael leaves as soon as the young Visagie begins to tell him what to do, and Michael repeats this pattern of leaving any time he finds himself in circumstances that require his participation in the master/servant dichotomy, however paradoxical and Hegelian that dichotomy may prove to be.

It is after Michael leaves the farm that he begins "the great hunger" that consumes him for the rest of the novel. Later, after he returns to the farm and replants his pumpkins, he digs a burrow in which he lives, and his hunger undergoes a transformation. In the hospital, he smells food and feels "the first hunger he had known for a long time" (71). But on the farm

> as he tended the seeds . . . and waited for the earth to bear food, his own need for food grew slighter and slighter. Hunger was a sensation he did not feel and barely remembered. If he ate, eating what he could find, it was because he had not yet shaken off the belief that bodies that do not eat die. (101)

When he finally eats a pumpkin, the act of eating becomes a ceremonious, reverent, and alternately cannibalistic sacrifice of the firstborn, indicative of the stillborn birth motif so characteristic of Coetzee's opus. While it is the best pumpkin he has ever eaten, and while "for the first time since he had arrived in the country he found pleasure in eating" (113), it is the act of creation, not the act of eating, that matters. But this act of creation, his cultivation and care of the land, like his persona, are constantly misinterpreted by the other characters in the novel; his tenuous cultivation of the future remains unrecognized by anyone participating in the dominant situation, the interregnum created by Coetzee's fictional civil war.

As I have stated earlier, this interregnum is marked by the social breakdown between the end, or the impending end, of one regime and the formation of another. Such a paradigm always perpetuates a dualistically defined reality. Just as there must be an old regime and a new for the interregnum to exist, there must also be oppressor and oppressed, masculine and feminine, human and animal, empire and nature. The space and time between such dualities is the "not yet" during which the future is unforeseeable. The concept of "not yet" pervades not only *Waiting for the Barbarians* but also *Life & Times of Michael K,* in which Michael's actions are always running up against the impossibility of transcending the present moment despite his continuous movement through boundaries in an attempt to exist "out of all the camps at the same time" (182). Two variables impact Michael's inability to escape the camps: the preponderance of the literal and figurative fences always forcing him to signify on one side or the other, and the absence of an active feminine principle, symbolized by the death of his mother, in the patriarchal enterprise of war. Michael can sense a pain only "obscurely connected with the future" (59), and therefore he "could not, or could *not yet*" (79, my emphasis) tell the story of his mother's ashes, just as, despite his reluctance to do so, he continues to eat because "he had *not yet* shaken off the belief that bodies that do not eat die" (101, my emphasis).

Furthermore, after he arrives at the farm, he thinks of his father as "the list of rules on the door of the dormitory" at Huis Norenius, while his "mother is buried and *not yet* risen" (104–5, my emphasis). In order to transcend the "not yet" of the interregnum, the mother or viable maternal principle, largely absent in all of Coetzee's works, must be restored. Otherwise Michael will remain caught in a situation where he realizes that while "it is not too late to run after [the soldiers who invade the farm], it is *not too late yet*" (111, my emphasis), he will remain unable to choose a side; it will always be chosen for him by anyone who attempts to read the text of starvation inscribed upon his body. This inability to choose, in large part, is a reaction to the binary logic that pervades the war-torn landscape from which Michael seeks to escape, a landscape that heightens the distinction between masculine and feminine and that enforces the arbitrary disjunction between culture and nature. Like the Magistrate, Michael is not incapable of imagination, but the time is not yet right for actual change: the language necessary for an alternate future—like the pumpkins Michael grows but must sacrifice—is not ready to be received into the current socio-political discourse.

Michael K, according to David Attwell, through protection, nourishment, and cultivation of the land attempts "to project a posthumanist, reconstructed ethics. . . . But the condition for such ethical reconstruction is a recognition of the pervasive intrusiveness of totalitarian violence" (*J. M. Coetzee* 97). This fictionalized South African state of affairs calls upon the oppressed to find a "new" or "minor" way (in Deleuze and Guatarri's sense), through actions that deny assimilation. But because ways of implementing change are highly inaccessible to the undernourished, the future state is impossible to envision, just as the South African future in *Life & Times of Michael K* is unclear. Michael will continue to hold out for the food that he is as yet unable to consume, but whether such food is forthcoming remains unknowable at the end of the narrative. Michael K continues to starve, but he is at least able to imagine possible survival by taking teaspoonfuls of water from the earth until the period of interregnum passes and a new age begins. Michael's starvation then symbolically allows for possibilities other than those that have currently been in place; as with any ritual, there is the possibility of transcending standard meaning. Michael K is still alive at the end of Coetzee's narrative, and while he does change in response to historical impositions, his transformation has no assimilative value; the change is imaginative, not external. This lack of assimilation is characteristic of minor texts "in their refusal to constitute the narrative as productive" (Lloyd 21). But despite this lack of canonical productivity, Michael K does not, at least by the end of the narrative, die the existential death of Kafka's hunger artist, the character upon which Coetzee no doubt models Michael, despite Coetzee's assertion that "I don't believe that Kafka has an exclusive right to the letter K. Nor is Prague the center of the universe" (qtd. In Morphet 457). Because Michael stops eating as a result of specific circumstances, he may resume eating at some unspecified future moment. Or he may, at some future point, like Kafka's hunger artist, starve to death regardless. However, there still exists the possibility for something other than death for Michael K. Even if he does so imaginatively, teaspoonful by teaspoonful, he may find the way in which "one can live" (184) to realize a post-interregnum future.

* * *

While the future has not yet arrived in either text, both Michael K and the Magistrate alter the interregnum narrative by placing themselves at odds with the discourse of war—either on an individual or mass scale—by refusing to signify either as active participants or conscientious objectors. Michael K, always attempting to escape, exists outside of such categorizations, while the Magistrate, interested in change from within, hovers between them. Acts of resistance are inscribed on the bodies of the protagonists in the form of blindness and hunger, both of which arise from ineffective purification rituals: the Magistrate ritually washes the body of the tortured barbarian girl entering deathlike spells, "or enchantment, blank, outside time" (31) as he attempts to obliterate the reality of her torture by becoming blind to it. Michael K becomes "smaller and harder and drier every day" (67) through a ritualized disordered consumption—anorexia—that constitutes another attempt at purification via a refusal to take into the body anything grown on the war-torn land. Neither ritual is particularly effective; of anorexia, Kim Chernin says, "much of the obsessive quality of an eating disorder arises precisely from the fact that food is being asked to serve a transformative function that it cannot carry by itself" (167). The same can be said of the Magistrate's obsessive, Lady Macbeth-like washing of the girl's body, of which he claims, "I suffer fits of resentment against my bondage to the ritual of oiling and rubbing" (41). Both behaviors, on a personal and private level, mimic both torture and war as rituals that take place in the political sphere.[3]

Furthermore, both characters become servants to these rituals and are controlled by behavior that they have invested with false, transformative power; the role of the imagination to create the possibility for an alternate scenario is transferred onto the ritual action, and the ritual fills the space left by an initial inability to imagine existence beyond the paradigm of war. In fact, in both cases, the line between purification and obliteration becomes increasingly contentious and is mediated by both characters' tendency to exist between life and death, in states of dreamless sleep where imagination is impossible. These states are "like death" (31) for the Magistrate and erase time for Michael: "through whole cycles of the heavens he slept . . . sometimes he would emerge into wakefulness unsure whether he had slept a day or a week or a month" (118–19). While such intermediate states allow for the kind of outside existence both characters seek, such escape can only be temporary and precludes any reciprocal relationships with other waking beings: in sleep, the Magistrate may be able to evoke an image of the face of the barbarian girl, but he will be unable to erase the waking truth of what was done to her. Similarly, Michael K may be able to cease eating while he sleeps, but he will eventually starve to death if he fails to eat when he is awake. When the Magistrate does dream, his dreams continually remind him of all he tries not to see and all he desperately seeks to forget. But the very persistence of the dreams points just as much to his inability to fully repress the reality of torture as a tool of Empire as to his inability to see, even on a subconscious level, the being and substance of the girl. He dreams repeatedly of a female child building a castle of snow, her back turned to him, and in his dreams, he attempts, unsuccessfully, to imagine the unimaginable: he tries "to imagine the face between the petals of her peaked hood but cannot" (10), and later, in a dream of "the figure [he calls] *the girl*," he says, "there are two shapes that arouse horror in me: massive and blank" (87). After he is tortured, however, he dreams of the girl, "wearing a round cap embroidered in gold" and with "clear jet-black eyes" (109). He can finally see the face of the girl, even if only an imaginary vision of how she might have appeared prior to her capture.

Elaine Scarry links her aforementioned discussion of hunger and imagined food to other forms of deprivation, specifically of human contact, and the imagined acquisition of companionship not only through the imagination, but also through dreams:

> Imagining a companion if the world provides none may . . . prevent longing from being a wholly self-experienced set of physical and emotional events that . . . exist as merely painful inner disturbances. It may be that "dreaming," too, should be understood in this way, as sustaining the objectifying powers of people . . . so that they do not during sleep drown in their own corporeal engulfment. (167)

Unlike the Magistrate whose dreamless sleep obliterates (and whose dreams alternately reconstitute) the girl and the extant regime that requires and allows for her torture, Michael K sleeps to obliterate the self. The narrative continually references Michael's status as a sleeper, supporting Robert's claim in the second part of the novel that "I have never seen anyone as asleep as you" (84). For Michael K, sleep is a refusal to engage with society, a return to the womb, and a resistance that begins at birth when the midwife notices his harelip, the initial reason for his continual hunger; as a baby, Michael has to be fed with a teaspoon because "the child could not suck from the breast" (3). Ultimately, it is the teaspoon that Michael imagines providing him with interregnum sustenance. This implement is the one way he is able to receive nourishment as a child, and it is the image of hope—the maternal care denied to him—that he can offer to a possible fellow traveler, who "K imagined . . . as a little old man with a stoop and a bottle in his side pocket who muttered all the time into his beard" (183). If this traveler, who functions as the only evidence of Michael's imagined potential, were to ask for water, the narrator tells us that Michael "would produce a teaspoon from his pocket" (184) with which to retrieve water from the well.

The Magistrate, in some unidentified outpost of Empire devoid of any temporal or historical markers, and Michael K, in a fictionalized South Africa that David Attwell says "exploits the unreality of the state's efforts at constitutional reform" through its policy of multinationalism during the early 1980s (*J. M. Coetzee* 91), both exist within parameters determined by war, their identities constantly defined in relation to some enigmatic "other" broadly defined as "the enemy." Despite historical influences on the latter novel, Michael K is placed within the framework of a fictional civil war in which he refuses to participate. This refusal is not born of any overt ethical or even conscious stance, but out of Michael's conviction that he is a gardener who must care for the land. According to Glennis Stephenson, in the harsh and repressive environment of Michael K, one "may be able to achieve . . . freedom only by leaving society and embracing a solitary elemental existence" (77). For Michael, the war that frames the narrative is fought between two unnamed groups that exist somewhere other than within the realm of Michael's acknowledgement; instead, conflict exists at the level of one-on-one relationships always in danger of taking on the trappings of war: "as soon as two or more people are together they will usually slip into the roles of master and servant, oppressor and oppressed" (Stephenson 80). Whenever the master/slave dynamic begins to make itself manifest in any interaction, Michael leaves, seeking a life of solitude and idleness that places him at odds with the society, order, and discipline sought by the Magistrate.

Michael seeks life outside of all structures that confine him and determine that his actions conform to any binary model that forces him to perform some service to fulfill the needs of another. In the Karoo, he thinks, "surely I have come as far as a man can come . . . surely now that in all the world only I know where I am, I can think of myself as lost" (66), and later he realizes that he is "learning to love idleness" (115). According to Moses, "the theme of idleness runs through Coetzee's fiction" (126), and Coetzee himself has commented on the European presentation of idleness among indigenous peoples in the early Discourse of the Cape. The idleness observed by colonizers among indigenous peoples, Coetzee claims, did not allow Europeans to compare or categorize the indigenous way of life, since idleness essentially resists categorization. Therefore, "condemning the Hottentot for his idleness, the early discourse of the Cape effectively excludes him from Eden by deciding that, though he is human, he is not in the line of descent that leads from Adam via a life of toil to civilized man" (*White Writing* 25). Michael's idleness and solitude, like his self-imposed starvation, place him outside of categorization by those who want to hear his story, positioning him instead as the barbarian beyond the reach of civilization, ironically and tellingly making him a victim of the forms of classification he seeks to avoid. Conversely, the Magistrate seeks society with the women who work in the kitchen, with the barbarian girl, and initially even with Colonel Joll by offering to take him "out fishing by night in a native boat" (1). Furthermore, while the Magistrate may tend a bit toward sloth, he does believe in the discipline provided by a code of conduct, however archaic and arbitrary that code may prove to be. While he does not favor the discipline of torture, a "technique . . . not an extreme expression of lawless rage" (Foucault 33) enforced by Joll, he does believe that the discipline of the law must prevail to bring about reparation—if any reparation is to be made—for the wrongs suffered by the "barbarians" as well as by himself.

Michael conceives of war as an unequal relationship between two individuals. The Magistrate, while acknowledging that the players in the war are made up of groups, similarly reduces them to two singular variables: the visible and pre-emptive military force of Empire and the forever threatening, imminently arriving, invisible barbarians. In both realities, the distinction between the duality of "us and them" that permeates the texts is determined by the fences that delineate the camps in which Michael K continually finds himself and by the gate that separates the Magistrate's compound from the land beyond its perimeter. The existence of fences create the existence of barbarians, and the placement of either group on the inside or the outside of the perimeter shifts depending on the context and is neither a fixed variable nor an essential truth; for the Magistrate, the barbarians are always beyond the gate, until he, through torture, signifies in the rhetoric of Empire as a barbarian himself. For Michael, the barbarian presence is confined within work and concentration camps, orphanages, and hospitals. Simply by virtue of the existence of such institutional barriers, neither the Magistrate nor Michael K is able to escape the reach of socially constructed divisions. In fact, after the Magistrate is tortured and later shown that "the gate is open" (125), he chooses to stay within the compound. Conversely, Michael may eventually get *outside,* but only if he passes through a series of locked gates, one fence seemingly enclosing another. After Michael escapes in Part Two of the novel, the medical officer claims that "the wire does not appear to have been cut; but then Michaels is enough of a wraith to slip through anything" (154). While both characters find themselves unable to transcend a reality that is still defined by fences—divisive structures that have not yet fallen into oblivion—both push at the boundaries that define their existence within the interregnum.

In the intermediate and external spaces occupied by the Magistrate and Michael, the only way to signify is through the suffering that they in some way choose for their bodies via an act of refusal. Such action distinguishes both characters from a more arbitrary suffering based instead on an individual's socially ascribed designation as "other." The Magistrate incurs torture when he refuses to confess, and Michael K fasts as he refuses confinement and seeks to exist "neither locked up nor standing guard at the gate" (182). Such suffering equalizes all bodies, male or female, black or white, by forcing the sufferer to identify with other bodies that have historically suffered, including, as I have previously stated, the bodies of animals. According to

Moses, at the level of the body in pain, the language that connects the Magistrate and the barbarian "proves indistinguishable from the subhuman roar of a tortured animal body. The mediated and prehistorical language of men and beasts naturally contains no discrete or articulate words; in such a tongue, the name of justice cannot be spoken" (127). Such a comment clearly privileges human speech over the "subhuman" speech—or roar—of the animal, a distinction that remains dependent upon the hierarchical thinking Coetzee's work often undermines and exposes as fallacious. It is worth noting that only in terms of the human condition is there any need for "the name of justice" to be spoken. Only humans can be unjust to animals and, by extension, to one another; to be like an animal within the context of these two novels is at once to be reduced to subhuman status and to exist outside of the proscriptions of human language. While the Magistrate does roar when he is tortured, Michael K is silent in the face of interrogations; as Mike Marais claims, "words, it would seem, rob K of his being and substance" ("Literature and Labour" 115). In the space between silence and the roar is language, the medium of communication that cannot be trusted as it problematizes access to the narrative of suffering whose text is the body.

* * *

Essentially, then, both novels have at their core a discourse of waiting: waiting for the confession, for the body of the barbarian girl to signify, for the end of the interregnum, for Michael's pumpkins to mature, and, of course, for the barbarians who may or may not be on their way. In the context of such waiting, according to Brian May, the body emerges as an ethical agent, and *Waiting for the Barbarians* "displays an ethical alternative to empire: a kind of waiting that represents at once the relaxation of the imperial will and the achievement of authentic openness to otherness" (414). As I have said in previous commentary, the animal body in Coetzee's work often signifies as itself and not as symbolic of something else. Similarly, as May suggests, human bodies, marked by suffering (torture in *Waiting for the Barbarians* or self-starvation in *Life & Times of Michael K*), signify for themselves as well:

> The body for Coetzee is not in itself so insignificant that it may be used merely as a means of characterizing something else. Worthy of characterization in its own right, the body is not just that which defies the mind . . . just as it is not simply that which is not. (May 393)

When the body signifies as a text readable in terms of its sufferings, it is meaningless to distinguish between human and animal bodies; the body is irreducible when it is in pain. As Moses states, if Coetzee's fiction embodies a "natural language unencumbered by the communal limits and historical mediation governing all linguistic systems in the postlapsarian age, it is, unfortunately, only the inarticulate speech of the body in pain" (126). But Brian May contends that "the body in Coetzee means not only pain, but possibility. It discloses, if nothing else, the possibility of disclosure" (415). Therefore, at the level of the body, there remains a possibility to exist outside the binary oppositions—including roar and silence—established and mediated by language. Such a space exists in the imagination, in imagined escape—through imagined food or companionship—from the pain inflicted upon and suffered by the body.

At the end of *Waiting for the Barbarians,* the Magistrate thinks "when we are cold and starving, or when the barbarian is truly at the gate, perhaps then I will abandon the locutions of a civil servant with literary ambitions and begin to tell the truth" (154). Such an assertion, dependent as it is on a sequence of potential occurrences including the arrival of a barbarian army whose very existence the Magistrate admits to doubt throughout the novel, assumes the existence of two problematic variables: some consistent notion of the "truth" and some clearly identifiable group that constitutes "barbarians." While the Magistrate claims that "perhaps" he will tell the truth at some unspecified future moment, Michael K claims that by taking spoonfuls of water from the earth, "one can live" (184). The uncertainty of the Magistrate's "perhaps" is replaced in *Life & Times of Michael K* with the definitive sense that one "can" live through the interregnum to see what lies beyond it. The "one" in question may or may not be Michael K; the text opens up the possibility for others to exist in Michael's imagined future. The use of the verb "can" at the end of the novel overrides the various "not yets" of the text, and signifies a belief rather than a possibility, a belief that would not be invoked by the use of the less certain "might." Therefore, Michael's admission that "one can live" as opposed to other possibilities—"one might live" or "I can live," for example—presupposes that someone will find a way through the interregnum, if the period of uncertainty does not drag on beyond a certain point. After all, one can live on water taken in spoonfuls from the earth, but not for long.

According to Emmanuel Levinas, suffering is "an excess, an unwelcome superfluity, that is inscribed in a sensorial content, penetrating . . . the dimensions of meaning that seem to open themselves to it, or become grafted onto it" (91). In *Waiting for the Barbarians* and *Life & Times of*

Michael K, torture, starvation, and imprisonment inscribe narratives of suffering on the various bodies that populate the texts, and both the Magistrate and Michael attempt, via unsuccessful purification rituals, to neutralize the causes of suffering, to return to a time before the suffering takes place, or to move beyond the interregnum after which such suffering will cease to exist. But in both novels, the continued existence of the inarticulate sound of a body in pain disrupts both characters' ability to escape into obliterative sleep: a fisherwoman's baby dies while she is held prisoner, and the Magistrate admits "how contingent my unease is, how dependent on a baby that wails beneath my window one night and does not wail the next," and the death "brings the worst shame to me, the greatest indifference to annihilation" (21). Similarly, when a young woman's baby cries in the night before dying at Jakkalsdrif, one of the labor camps in which Michael is interred, Michael, "aching to sleep," wishes "the child annihilated" (87–88). For both the Magistrate and Michael, the sleep they desperately seek is like death, "an oblivion, a nightly brush with annihilation" (*Waiting* 21), the escape from the suffering of the body. For the infants in both novels, death is the only escape from suffering, and death, if there is redemption to be found in either novel, is the option that neither the Magistrate nor Michael is willing—as of yet—to accept. But the crying of the child is disruptive, a reminder that there must be accountability, and the death of the child is an ominous marker of the present, the lack of fecundity and reproductive promise in the holding pattern of the interregnum.

Chapter Five

The Performance of Displacement:
Disgrace and *The Lives of Animals*

Identifying with a gender under contemporary regimes of power involves identifying with a set of norms that are and are not realizable, and whose power and status precede the identifications by which they are insistently approximated. This "being a man" and this "being a woman" are internally unstable affairs. They are always beset by ambivalence precisely because there is a cost in every identification, the loss of some other set of identifications, the forcible approximation of a norm one never chooses, a norm that chooses us, but which we occupy, reverse, resignify to the extent that the norm fails to determine us completely. (Judith Butler, *Bodies that Matter* 126–7)

Saying . . . is performative, interlocutory . . . a relational process rather than a fixed relationship; it is movement, not stasis; it reaches toward an infinite future (or further Saying), rather than recording a past interaction or history (the Said). Violent adequation of the Other is precluded because the Other remains outside the limits of comprehension, outside of history, un-Said. (James Meffan and Kim L. Worthington on Emmanuel Levinas, "Ethics before Politics: J. M. Coetzee's *Disgrace*" 136).

In *Disgrace* (1999), the waiting that informs South African fiction of the 1980s, including Coetzee's *Waiting for the Barbarians* and *Life & Times of Michael K* has come to an end, and the reader is positioned squarely in the "now" beyond the "not yet" of the interregnum that characterizes those earlier works. *Disgrace* is situated "in this place, at this time" (112), South Africa at the current post-apartheid moment, and centers around the disgrace of

David Lurie, a white South African academic who is forced to resign from his university teaching position after he engages in a questionably consensual sexual relationship with a young female student. After his resignation, Lurie leaves Cape Town to live with his daughter, Lucy, in the Eastern Cape and to work at the Animal Welfare League with Bev Shaw, a middle-aged woman who euthanizes some of South Africa's superfluous pet and livestock population. In terms of Coetzee's literary opus, the lesbian character of Lucy is the culmination of both the Magistrate and Michael K's modes of resistance in the 1980s-era texts mentioned above: as the feminine principle that denies male determinism, she is a woman who works for change from within as opposed to outside of existing structures, a gardener who, unlike her predecessor, Michael K, is able to partake of the tentative "bread of freedom" that she grows on the land she shares with Petrus, a black man who helps her care for the dogs she kennels. Such "freedom" is complex and uncertain, and when three black men rape Lucy, she proclaims her decision not to report the crime a "private matter" (112). As an experience about which she will share no confession, her silence ends when she discovers that she is pregnant with a child she refuses to abort. Therefore, *Disgrace* leaves us with two aspects that were impossible for Coetzee to depict more than a decade earlier: a living (yet co-opted) garden and a living (yet unborn) child.

In *Disgrace,* David Lurie, a "representative of the dislocated post-apartheid white writer" (Poyner 68), is displaced by virtue of his status as white, academic, and male in a political context that no longer treats such attributes as definitive. Furthermore, by virtue of an illicit sexual relationship with a young female student named Melanie, Lurie is displaced (and disgraced) when he is driven from a university that will not "in this day and age" (44)—post-apartheid South Africa—tolerate such behavior, especially given Lurie's refusal to grant a confession of any wrongdoing despite his admission of guilt and his claim that he is a "servant of Eros" (52). But after Lucy's rape on her smallholding in the Eastern Cape, it becomes impossible to view David's interaction with Melanie as mere seduction, his treatment of her as anything other than the "abuse" (53) of which he is accused by a female member of the university disciplinary committee. In *Disgrace,* women's bodies signify as sites of displacement; for the black men who rape her, Lucy's white female body symbolizes the land from which they have been dispossessed. For David, Melanie's biracial female body offers the opportunity to symbolically reclaim not only his youth, but also his authoritarian position at a university where the white male professor is marginalized by increasing institutional demands for gender and racial diversification. But at its core, *Disgrace* is a novel about a performance, or rather two performances, David Lurie's and J. M. Coetzee's:

because he is present but "offstage," locked in the bathroom during his daughter's rape, Lurie later attempts to imagine, through the writing of an operatic performance, the trauma experienced by Lucy. For Coetzee, present through persistent questions asked by the narrative voice, yet also "offstage" as the author of a metafictional novel, female bodies in *Disgrace* allow for a narrative performance about the limitations of the sympathetic imagination. After his daughter's rape, David embarks upon the perhaps impossible quest to embody the other—in the form of black South Africans, women, and animals—through the medium of a specific staged performance, an opera he struggles to write (but tellingly never completes) for Byron's one time lover, Teresa.

Disgrace has been treated harshly by some critics who feel that the novel contributed nothing positive to representations of the post-apartheid status of the "new" South Africa. In a 2003 article in *Scrutiny2*, Colin Bower claims, "I simply cannot see how . . . David Lurie can be taken as anything less than repellent," and, within a twenty-page critical examination of Coetzee's work, ironically finds Lurie (as well as the rest of Coetzee's opus) "quite unworthy of any sort of critical attention" (14). According to Salman Rushdie, the novel's damning weakness is the inability of its characters to understand one another: "Lurie does not understand Lucy . . . and she finds his deeds beyond her;" furthermore, "whites don't understand blacks, and the blacks aren't interested in understanding the whites" (A19). However contentious Rushdie's claim may be—one could argue that the only character who does not understand anyone else is David Lurie since the novel is focalized through his point of view—a lack of understanding in "this place, at this time" is the necessary product of a postcolonial and post-apartheid narrative about shifting and renegotiated power in an historical moment fraught with various racially and sexually determined displacements. Furthermore, such critical dismissals can be read as evidence of a refusal by the critic to engage dialogically with the dilemma of identification posed by Coetzee in the novel itself.

The displacements that characterize Coetzee's narratives—including the free indirect discourse of *Disgrace*—serve to shed light on subject positions that the author does not occupy by presenting the interaction of multiple subjectivities as performed dialogue between not only the characters within the novel, but also between the inquisitive third-person narrative voice and the reader, who must attempt to pose some answers. Coetzee, therefore, as I have claimed earlier in this study, writes dialogically in the Bahktinian sense, as one who refuses to claim the narrative position of the monologic insider, the textual presence that has access to contested notions of the truth. In *Disgrace,* David Lurie attempts to imagine the subjectivity of his daughter after her rape, a task that is revealed through what I will call "dialogic drag" by Coetzee's performance of the narrative position of Elizabeth Costello in *Elizabeth Costello* (2003), a work that comprises various lectures presented by Coetzee and attributed to the fictional, feminist novelist for whom the collection is named. Such attempts at imagined identification with the other, we learn from Elizabeth Costello's example, will always result in a performance that parodies the "real." Included in *Elizabeth Costello* is *The Lives of Animals* (1999), a work that, because of the fact that its separate publication as a philosophical text/novella immediately preceded the publication of *Disgrace* and because of its implicit/explicit animal rights narrative, is often read as a "companion piece" to that novel.

Judith Butler claims that "drag is a site of a certain ambivalence, one which reflects the more general situation of being implicated in the regimes of power by which one is constituted and hence being implicated in the very regime one opposes" ("Gender" 125). As a form of displacement and renegotiation of power, she claims that drag is not always a form of ridicule nor is it merely a way of "passing" as something that one is not. Furthermore, and perhaps most important to a study of *Disgrace* and *The Lives of Animals,* drag is not exclusively the realm of male, homosexual performance. The performance of a gendered position, however, is an attempt to understand the ununderstandable aspects—or alterity—of the other, and as such illustrates an exercise in the enactment of the sympathetic imagination. The concept of performing the other has value in an examination of Emmanuel Levinas's notion of alterity as exemplified by his conception of the Saying and the Said that are described in the epigraph to this chapter, a discourse often invoked by Coetzee's critics with regard to both *Disgrace* and *The Lives of Animals.* While much has been written about the alterity of animals in both works,[1] no critic has examined the performative aspects of these works as a dual exercise—both for David Lurie in *Disgrace* via the opera he writes, and for Coetzee via Elizabeth Costello, the elderly, feminist novelist whose voice speaks his 1997–98 Tanner Lectures in *The Lives of Animals*—in the enactment of trauma experienced in the lives of others.

In the Freudian sense, according to Ariella Azoulay, "trauma . . . is given its meaning only when it is experienced a second time, only in retroactive fashion when it is articulated and told to an addressee" (34–35), or, I would contend, only when it is re-enacted and thereby performed before an audience. Azoulay argues that in *Disgrace,* Lucy's rape (the second rape) becomes the narrative articulation of Melanie's rape (the first rape). It is the second violation that reveals the trauma of the first, a trauma often unrecognized by many of

Coetzee's critics who, according to Lucy Graham, dismiss the incident between Lurie and Melanie as an affair. Such an interpretation is understandable given that the narrative of the "relationship" is written through Lurie as a focalizer, but according to Graham, "although Lurie protests to the contrary, the act he commits is rape" (7). Whether Lurie protests is questionable; it is perhaps more accurate to say that no character in the novel, like many of Coetzee's critics, questions the narrative voice in its biased assertions. For example, the narrative interpretation of Melanie's smile as "sly" instead of "shy" (11) should be suspect given David's desire to view Melanie's complicity with regard to their sexual encounters. Only by recognizing parallels between the two young women, Melanie and Lucy—the first non-white, the second white—and the parallels between the white David Lurie and the black rapists in the latter part of the novel is the reader able to recognize David's earlier encounters with Melanie as instances of violation. Similarly, the performative aspects of *Disgrace* (the latter text) can be revealed by an analysis of the overt performance of female enactment in the Costello lectures in general, especially in *The Lives of Animals* (the previous text).

In the pair of lectures she presents at the fictional Appleton College that comprise *The Lives of Animals,* the female persona of Elizabeth Costello—"a Coetzean figure" (Poyner 73)—compares the Holocaust in Germany to the treatment of animals in industrialized societies. The character of Elizabeth Costello has also been performed by Coetzee in other lectures as well including the 1996 Ben Belitt Lecture at Bennington College, "What is Realism?"; the 1998 Una's Lecture at the University of California, Berkeley, "The Novel in Africa"; and the 2002 Nexus Conference Lecture in the Netherlands, "Elizabeth Costello and the Problem of Evil." In October of 2003, just after Coetzee was awarded the Nobel Prize in literature, he gave the Troy Lecture at the University of Massachusetts, Amherst. His reading, "At the Gate," along with the other Costello lectures listed above are constituents of the "Eight Lessons" that comprise the novel *Elizabeth Costello.* In each of these narratives, Costello/Coetzee explicitly acknowledges the role of performance in the construction and presentation of the multi-faceted, non-fictional lectures presented via a fictional persona through a non-fictional author about works of fiction. As Costello tells fictional Nigerian novelist Emmanuel Egundu after he presents a exposition of the role of the body in uniquely African oral literature, "what you seem to be demanding is not just a voice but a performance: a living actor before you, performing your text" ("The Novel" 13). Coetzee addresses the author's role as a performer of the narrative by disrupting his own presentation of Elizabeth Costello's argument in "What is Realism?" by claiming that despite the fact that "generally speaking it is not a good idea to interrupt the narrative too often," he must skip certain aspects of her story in the interest of time: "the skips are not part of the text," he claims, "they are part of the performance" (68) in the context of a postmodern moment when, according to the voice of Costello, "[writers] are just performers, speaking our parts" ("What is" 71). In the context of the Costello lectures, to embody is to perform, and the acknowledgement of the mimicry inherent in the performance of another gender is also an acknowledgement of the limitations of the sympathetic imagination, the enactment that will never be "the real"—a concept that Coetzee finds contentious, anyway—but will always be, at best, a parody.

In *Disgrace,* the third-person narrative voice asks of David, "does he have it in him to be the woman?" (160) as he attempts, unsuccessfully, to imagine Lucy's rape from her perspective. David, seeming to recognize—however obtusely—the argument posed by Elizabeth Costello in *The Lives of Animals,* does ultimately empathize with the bodily suffering his daughter endures by unconsciously placing the rape of women in an analogous relationship to the slaughter of livestock animals. After Lucy's rape, David forms a bond with two Persian sheep that Petrus plans to slaughter, and he is disinclined to eat them because, without any reason that he can discern, "their lot has become important to him" (126). While David never actively participates in a vegetarian ethic, his sensibility with regard to the lives of animals is greatly altered after Lucy is raped, and this change in perception results from a respect for the being of animals regardless of whether or not David can access the animal's interiority. In *Disgrace,* unlike Coetzee's earlier works, the animal—specifically and as usual, the dog—is central to the narrative action as opposed to influentially peripheral. If *The Lives of Animals* is Coetzee's performative parody of an academic, vegetarian woman, Elizabeth Costello, who asserts the highly problematic claim that as a writer of fiction, she does have it in her to *be* an animal: "if I can think my way into the existence of a being who has never existed, then I can think my way into the existence of a bat or a chimpanzee or an oyster" (35), then *Disgrace* is Coetzee's critique of the vanity of such claims about the sympathetic imagination: at best, as David discovers—whether he is aware of his discovery or not—one can mimic or parody the subjectivity of the other, but to claim that one can actually be or "think [one's] way into the existence" of another is arrogant indeed. And Coetzee, through the character of Susan Moebius, makes this point in "What is Realism?" When Elizabeth Costello's son John tells Susan that in her fiction, "my mother has been a man . . . she has also been a dog," Susan counters, "it's just mimicry. Women are good at mimicry, better than men. At parody, even" (73). If we subvert this claim and take Susan at her word, then Coetzee's embodiment of Elizabeth Costello can be read as the parody that must inform David's attempts to "be" Lucy in *Disgrace*.

Much recent criticism of *Disgrace*, with its attention to the role of secular confession in a world "in the absence of grace" (Graham 4) where "animals and art provide the substance of Lurie's new existence" (Attridge, "Age of Bronze" 108), can be read in defense of its bleak and seemingly negative portrayal of a post-apartheid South Africa where whites, and particularly white women, become victims of black vengeance. Jane Poyner reads the novel "as an allegory of the Truth [and Reconciliation] Commission within the framework of (secular) confession" (67), while Mike Marais, James Meffan, and Kim L. Worthington tease out a discourse of Levinas's concept of alterity as it pertains to Coetzee's treatment of the other. Marais defends Coetzee's respect for the alterity of the other by claiming that "in reflecting on its failure to represent the other, the text reflects on the excession of the other. The point here is that the text's failure to instantiate the other is also a failure to *eliminate* the other" ("The Possibility" 60–61). Meffan and Worthington argue that Lurie's act of self-reflective doubt, inherent when the narrator asks, "does he have it in him to be the woman?" may be ethically productive, a "question whose terms recognize another's perhaps insurmountable alterity" (144). The essential point extrapolated by Coetzee's critics with regard to Levinasian philosophy deals with the notion that one can never fully comprehend the other and must respect the alterity—or insurmountable difference—of the other despite the impossibility of imagined identification with the other. Such respect begins with self-questioning inherently located in the act of "Saying": "the Spirit is not the Said, it is the Saying which goes from the Same to the Other, without suppressing the difference. It paves a way for itself where there is nothing in common" (Levinas 63). But Levinas's notion of alterity is applicable only to other humans and fails to encompass the various non-human others that populate all of Coetzee's narratives.

Various critics read the role of animals in *Disgrace* as the means by which David Lurie begins to learn to love the other—the "absolute other" (Attridge, "Age of Bronze" 114)—by taking responsibility for the bodies of dead dogs despite the fact, as Lucy Graham claims, "that Lurie's work in the service of dead dogs is not redemptive in itself" (11). Derek Attridge claims that *Disgrace* is not so much about postcolonial South Africa as it is about the cultural colonization of South Africa by the West: the novel is a portrayal of "a new global age of performance indicators and outcomes measurement, of bench marking and quality assurance, of a widespread prurience that's also an unfeeling puritanism" (105), and Louise Bethlehem points to the theatrical way that the text deals with these conflicting notions of prurience and puritanism when she says, "if the rape of Lucy takes place *offstage* . . . then so too does the *enactment* of her sexual pleasure" (22, my emphasis). While such a claim clearly points to the absence of Lucy's narrative perspective that would allow her to confess either trauma or joy, it also alludes to the ways that the text is staged by Coetzee and performed by the characters that populate it.

Furthermore, David, in his attempts to imagine Lucy's rape from her perspective, constructs a fictionalized narrative of her experience—as she claims, David treats her as if all of her actions are "part of the story of [his] life" (198)—that runs up against his work on Byron, "something for the stage. . . . Characters talking and singing" (63). In fact, *Disgrace* is filled with references to various theaters, performances, and enactments, stagings of narratives that are never completed and that ultimately parody the truth of what they attempt to portray. When Lurie asks Melanie about her studies, she tells him that she is getting a "diploma in theatre" (14). And when he watches her rehearsing the play, *Sunset at the Globe Salon,* "a comedy of the new South Africa set in a hairdressing salon" (23), he becomes the unknown voyeur of her enactment of a character within the play within Coetzee's staging of David's narrative. David is drawn to the character, the "apparition" (25), Melanie becomes as he watches her perform. The play, in David's opinion, is ridiculous: "all the coarse old prejudices [are] brought into the light of day and washed away in gales of laughter" (23), and when he goes to see the performance again at the end of the novel, he finds its crass humor and overtly political message "as hard to endure as before"(191). Humor and humility, however, are what he ultimately depends upon, as he uses Lucy's banjo—an instrument created and first played by black Africans[2]—to hybridize and shape his own historical narrative of the middle-aged Teresa, an Italian aristocrat who "looks more like a peasant" (181), more, in fact, like Lucy's friend Bev Shaw than Melanie.

The transition from writing about Byron for whom he can find words to writing about Teresa, "young, greedy, willful, petulant" (181) for whom he cannot, takes place after his altercation with Melanie, a woman he imagines as similarly young, willful, and demanding. But the focus of his theatrical endeavor shifts again to Teresa in middle-age after he meets Bev Shaw, the "remarkably unattractive" (82), middle-aged woman who euthanizes South Africa's unwanted animals. Initially glib about his feelings for animals and his consumption of them ("do I like animals? I eat them so I suppose I must like them" (81)), David ultimately becomes completely transfixed by what happens in the "theatre" (143) of the Animal Welfare League, the staging and dramatic enactment of a kind of ritualized and honorable death for animals—mainly dogs—at the hands of Bev Shaw. Of Teresa, and I would argue of Bev, the narrator asks, "can he find it in his heart to love this plain, ordinary woman?" (182), a question that provides a kind of answer to the earlier question after Lucy's rape: while David may not ever be able to "be" the woman, he may possibly come to love a woman who is ordinary, not young, and who may be able to guide him in a productive direction. He realizes the limits of imagined identification with Lucy and comes to accept that the best he can do or the closest he can approximate is dialogic drag, a mimetic parody of an unrepresentable alterity: "this is how it must be from here on: Teresa giving voice to her lover, and [David] . . . giving voice to Teresa" (183)—while Coetzee gives voice to him. The voice of the man (Byron) is mediated through the voice of the woman (Teresa) as it is mediated through the voice of man (David) in *Disgrace*. While David wants to let Teresa tell her story of Byron, the story she can tell in his opera is still only the story that he writes for her, the narrative he imagines being performed by another woman, an actor, who will be neither Teresa nor his idea of her. That David is never able to complete his opera illustrates both a failure of the sympathetic imagination and, conversely, a testament to an unarticulated understanding that the alterity of the other, in his case Teresa, is never representable, never successfully performed.

In a moment that harkens back to the seeming ridiculousness David critiques after viewing *Sunset at the Globe Salon,* he realizes the impossibility of attempting to voice Teresa in the context of the South African here and now. When he examines his own apparent absurdity as he "sits among the dogs singing to himself" (212) while three black boys from D Village watch him over the fence, he questions whether it would be permissible to allow an animal into the play to voice its own story. After all, a narrative of trauma inflicted upon animal bodies that come "nowhere" (73) on the list of South Africa's priorities after the fall of apartheid is more relevant, certainly, than the story of Teresa's lost love: "would he dare . . . bring a dog into the piece . . . ? Why not? Surely, in a work that will never be performed, all things are permitted?" (215). Such questions are characteristic of the text after Lucy's rape as the narrative perspective shifts from a voice of relative certainty to a voice that challenges the validity and veracity of David's choices, beliefs, and conceptions of the self. Such questioning, according to Meffan and Worthington, is perhaps ethically productive because it points to David's realization of the limits of his own perception, but "what will gall the reader, and probably incite new criticism of Coetzee's quietism," they claim, "is his refusal in *Disgrace* to do more than suggest the need to ask new questions of the self" (146). For the most part, however, the questions that the narrative asks are not questions that David asks of himself but are instead questions the third-person narrator asks about David's position in the narrative. From the narrator's question, "does he have it in him to be the woman?" follow others: after asking, "can he find it in his heart to love this plain, ordinary woman [Teresa in middle age]?" (182), the narrator later asks, how he can justify, in the context of the current historical moment, "what Teresa and her lover have done to deserve being brought back to this world" (212). But one of the only questions that David asks of himself is about animals and about his revulsion to eating meat after Lucy's rape.

As I have noted throughout this study, the colonial impulse to treat people like animals is apparent in all of Coetzee's works beginning with *Dusklands* in which Jacobus claims "death is as obscure to [the bushman] as to an animal" (80). Coetzee deconstructs such othering in *Boyhood* when the autobiographical character of John becomes averse to the aesthetic of meat and in *Life & Times of Michael K* when Michael's hunger for the ethical begins with the slaughter of a goat and ends with a purely vegetarian—albeit minimal—mode of consumption. In *Disgrace,* when Petrus tethers two sheep to a bare patch of ground days before he plans to slaughter them, David becomes agitated and advocates for their removal to a place where they might graze. When he ponders the bond that has formed between himself and the sheep, the narrative lets the reader inside of David's thoughts: "do I have to change, *he thinks?* Do I have to become like Bev Shaw?" (126, my emphasis). Earlier in the novel, we learn that Lucy is a longtime vegetarian who "refuses to touch meat" (121), but David's aversion to meat begins to take shape, for reasons he cannot fully understand, only after Lucy is raped. When she asks him if he has changed his mind about the way he feels about animals, he claims, "no. . . . Nevertheless, in this case I am disturbed. I can't say why" (127). When he does eat the mutton at Petrus's party, he tells himself that he will ask for forgiveness later. Despite the fact that David cannot say what brings about this particular disturbance, the connections between the bodies of women and animals are apparent within the text; David, therefore, may not be able to "be" the woman—his daughter, Teresa, or Melanie—but he seems to be able, at least on a physical level, to empathize with the trauma inflicted on women through rape by recognizing, through his body in the form of its revulsion to meat, the trauma inflicted on animals through slaughter. Such a recognition occurs outside the realm of the imagination; it is an instinctive reaction and is therefore legitimate in ways that transcend thought and philosophy. In a rhetorical context, women are treated "like meat" when they are raped, a metaphor that underscores David's subsequent relationships with animals who literally become meat when they are killed.

Of this connection, Carol J. Adams asks in *The Sexual Politics of Meat,* "what connects being a receptacle and being a piece of meat, being entered and being eaten?" and answers, "if you are a piece of meat, you are subject to a knife, to implemental violence" (54). Lucy articulates the connection between woman, animal, and meat when she confronts David about his similarity to the men who raped her:

> When you have sex with someone strange—when you trap her, hold her down, get her under you, put all your weight on her—isn't it a bit like killing? Pushing the knife in; exiting afterwards, leaving the body behind covered in blood—doesn't it feel like murder, like getting away with murder? (158)

David, despite his inability to make the connection between his rape of Melanie and this rape of Lucy, can identify with the rapists and also employs the language of consumption when he imagines how the men must have felt as they raped Lucy and "drank up her fear" (160). In terms of rape, the body of woman becomes so closely elided with the rhetoric of meat that the animal, according to Adams, becomes an "absent referent" because "animals in name and body are made absent *as animals* for meat to exist" (40). In *Disgrace*, David's question to himself about whether he must change and become like Bev does two extremely productive things: first, within the context of the novel, it illustrates a shift (or at the very least the potential for a shift) in David's thinking about Bev in particular and women in general. If he is inclined to be more "like Bev"—and by being disturbed by the slaughter sheep, he has become more like her (whatever this may mean) than he may be prepared to admit—then he may be more inclined to be guided by a woman's compassion than "enriched" (56) by a physical relationship with her.[3] Secondly, he restores the absent referent of the animal to the text and, through the animal, can form an empathetic identification with the woman—or at least with Lucy, who has been treated like an animal by a group of people—black South African men—who have, in turn, historically been treated like animals within the context of South African colonial history.

The body of the animal, then, in particular the body of the dog that David "sacrifices" at the end of the narrative is a dog, not a symbolic representation of Lucy or of any of the other characters in the novel. While David's "giving up" of the animal can be read as his "giving up" of his daughter, it is through the dog himself that David learns to give without expecting anything in return. David can love the dog, will do for the dog "when his time comes" (220) because he has accepted responsibility for the dog as a being inherently entitled to love. This reciprocity, this "less than little: nothing" (220), in its potential for ethical productivity, is, in many ways, utterly promising. Lucy agrees to marry Petrus and give him her land in return for his protection, and David is appalled at Lucy's decision to place herself in a position he views as humiliating, as a person forced to live "like a dog" (205). But for Lucy, this is a place of beginning, a place to "start from again" (205). By leveling the post-apartheid playing field and placing everyone in the position of the dog, Coetzee rewrites Franz Kafka's existential ending in *The Trial* when Joseph K proclaims his fate to be "like a dog" (231) and renders literal the condition of both humans and animals in the new South Africa: for change to occur, it would seem, everyone must begin again from the same place, with the liberation of the land from its contested historical status. To begin "like a dog" is simply to start over, and the literary and historically negative connotation of this famous and persistent simile is itself essentially negated.

Lucy, therefore, may be able to imagine living "like a dog" even though David is unable to "be the woman," to imaginatively perform the characters of Teresa or Lucy or even Bev. In fact, the one woman whose subjectivity David can imagine is another woman, like David's Teresa, written into being by a man, namely Gustav Flaubert's Madame Bovary.[4] Early in the novel after an encounter with the prostitute Soraya, David imagines himself as "Emma Bovary, coming home . . . from an afternoon of reckless fucking" (5), and later in the novel, after he first sleeps with Bev, he thinks of her as "Emma Bovary strutting before the mirror after her first big afternoon. I have a lover! I have a lover! sings Emma to herself" (150). Emma Bovary, the fictional woman imagined by a man, becomes the fictional woman enacted by David Lurie in his relationship with Soraya and the fictional conceit he uses to imagine Bev Shaw—herself a fictional woman imagined by another man, Coetzee—and her delight in their sexual encounter. If David can be any woman, she is only the woman interpreted through the gaze of another man: Byron, Flaubert, or Coetzee.

When Joanna Scott asked Coetzee what it meant for him to write from the perspective of his female narrator Magda in *In the Heart of the Country* (1982), he answered,

> A complicated question. One way of responding is to ask, is one, as a writer, at every level sexed? Is there not a level where one is, if not presexual, then anterior to sex? First anterior to sex, then becoming sexed? At that level, or in that transition between levels, does one actually "take on" the voice of another sex? Doesn't one "become" another sex? (91)

As an answer, this one seems particularly evasive and provocative, illustrative of Coetzee's ability to question, if not state a firm belief in, the notion that the writer must at the very least attempt to embody and perform other subjectivities. Scott's question mirrors the narrator's question of David Lurie in *Disgrace:* "does he have it in him to be the woman?" (160), and the answer to this question, when one looks at the performative nature of *Disgrace,* is a resounding—but not at all negatively connoted—no.

* * *

In an article on the Truth and Reconciliation Commission in which she refers to *The Lives of Animals,* Jacqueline Rose says, "intellectuals are always accused of talking too much, not acting enough" (178). Rose's statement first speaks to the seeming disjunction between intellectualism and activism, between the spoken and the enacted, but it is also worth exploring the use of the verb "to act," meant in Rose's case, I am sure, in its kinetic sense, to respond physically to a set of given stimuli—apartheid, the threat of war with Iraq, or factory farming, for example. But "acting" in the Costello lectures is a performative understanding that involves Coetzee's mimetic exercise in embodiment, the manifestation of imagined identification—with fictional characters, with animals, and with women. For example, in *The Lives of Animals,* Coetzee's 1997–8 Princeton Tanner Lectures, Coetzee addresses the ethics of meat-eating and animal experimentation via the persona of fictional, feminist novelist, Elizabeth Costello, a character who delivers two lectures, "disconcertingly like the Tanner Lectures" (Gutman 3), on animal rights at Appleton College. As an intellectual figure, Costello is also an activist who lives her ethics by virtue of her vegetarianism, and Coetzee performs Costello who acts when she refuses to eat meat. Furthermore, Coetzee acted as he stood before his audience at Princeton and performed Costello, embodied her position, imagined his way "into the existence of a being who never existed," and posited an extremely problematic analogy, that factory farming is like the Holocaust.

Costello's analogy is so radical, in fact, her rhetoric so inflammatory and visceral, filled with phrases like "hacked flesh" and "death wounds," that the audience—her own within Coetzee's text and Coetzee's outside in the "real" world—recoils at what she herself refers to as the "cheap point-scoring" (22) of her argument. The audience, at least from a critical perspective, has tended to write her out of the narrative. Ultimately and most vehemently, literary critics either repeatedly posit her fictionality, overdetermining the seemingly obvious fact that she is not Coetzee, or they conflate author and character, attributing the animal rights argument not to Costello but to Coetzee. The reason for the silencing of Costello is the critics' inability to recognize the performative aspects of Coetzee's text, attributable at least in part to Coetzee's tendency to disrupt conventional notions of genre. How do we categorize lectures like *The Lives of Animals,* and how do we categorize *Elizabeth Costello,* the collected version of these lectures, a work that Judith Shulevitz claims is "less than a novel but much more than a collection of stories" (15)? Is *The Lives of Animals,* published in 1999 as a slight anthology that contained not only the two lectures that comprise *The Lives of Animals,* but also several critical essays by animal rights philosophers and literary critics, a work of fiction or, because of the performative format in which it was initially delivered, is it Coetzee's argumentative truth presented in the guise of an analysis of the sympathetic imagination? Coetzee's embodiment of Elizabeth Costello can be read as a parody of an elderly woman with a rigid and moralistic sensibility who believes, as she claims in "The Problem of Evil," that "to save our humanity, certain things we may want to see . . . must remain off-stage" (57) in the fictitious (re)enactment and performance of literature. But to read Costello as mere parody undermines the role she plays with regard to the questions the self must ask of the self in the service of the Levinasian concept of the Saying. If Costello is the answer to Coetzee's question of male embodiment of the feminine persona, the question the narrator of *Disgrace* asks of David, then the questions she raises in Coetzee's audience—questions about ethics, embodiment, and the other—refuse answers of easy appropriation.

Elizabeth Costello is a fictional character constructed by J. M. Coetzee, just as Coetzee is, more often than not, a fiction constructed by his critics. Despite the fact that Costello's voice may not be Coetzee's, neither is Costello's voice her own. The character of Elizabeth Costello, her argument that people treat animals the way the Nazis treated the Jews, and Coetzee's rendering of both of these variables, establishes a third and perhaps more sentimental place from which to write against the primary binary opposition of animal/human. In terms of its dualistic connotations, "sentimentality" is excessive, female, emotional, and hard to attribute to Coetzee. As critics, we would much rather attribute it to Costello because it is easier to portray her reasoning as flawed, to find her excessive, just as Abraham Stern does when he refuses to break bread with Costello claiming, "the Jews died like cattle, therefore cattle die like Jews, you say. That is a trick of words that I will not accept" (49). Yet it is precisely a "trick of words," the disruptive and non-normative form that Coetzee employs, that makes *The Lives of Animals* so polemical, and it is a trick of gender that makes critics want to distance Coetzee from

Elizabeth Costello. Clearly, we cannot equate Costello and Coetzee just as Stern cannot equate cattle and Jews, and Peter Singer, in his struggle to make sense of Costello's position, says in an essay that follows *The Lives of Animals,* "a comparison is not necessarily an equation" (86). But what is striking is a pervasive need by critics to posit Costello's fictionality, or at the very least, to read her metaphorically. According to Michael Bell, Costello provides Coetzee a way of getting things done; for Bell, "*Lives* provides a study of why Coetzee cannot readily believe in 'believes in'" ("What is it Like"). Similarly, David Attwell claims that Costello is a surrogate for Coetzee, a reprisal; she is like Erasmus's fool ("The Lives and Times"). According to Attwell, Costello makes a case for the sympathetic imagination, a concept whose limits are critiqued by Sam Durrant's discussion of the ethics of stupidity and Dominic Head's claim of irony in Costello's ability to reason "that reason is less valuable than sympathy" ("The Limits of Empathy"). Furthermore, the animal rights argument, presented by Costello as presented by Coetzee, is also read metaphorically, according to Michael Bell, as "a Trojan horse designed to deconstruct the nature of conviction in relation to fundamental life issues such as the Shoah, or apartheid" ("What is it Like")

To claim that Coetzee is not Costello is to state the obvious for various reasons, not the least of which is that Costello is a fictional female character, and given what we do know about South African history, it is probably safe to assume that Coetzee feels a certain and understandable degree of unease voicing his subject position, a South African masculinity complicated by the variable of whiteness. As I have stated previously in this study, the white female voice, as the voice of the boundary keeper, both oppressed by and complicit with the colonial project, is a more authentic place from which Coetzee can speak. *Disgrace* poses an interesting counterpoint to the Coetzee-is-not-Costello debate because despite the fact that both Coetzee and protagonist David Lurie are male and both teach or have taught university-level literature in Cape Town, critics do not concern themselves with setting up a distinction between these two; we seem more readily to accept that Coetzee and Lurie are distinct personas, and the "laws" that govern readings of fiction forbid us from doing something as reductive as conflating the positions of author and protagonist. Or perhaps such an option is never considered because Coetzee does not perform Lurie even as Lurie attempts to perform the various women who people his narrative. According to Butler, "the speech act is a bodily act, and . . . the force of the performative is never fully separable from bodily force" (*Excitable* 141). Therefore, my goal with regard to *The Lives of Animals* is to talk about the distinct persona of Elizabeth Costello as the imagined body through which Coetzee enacts emotional speech.

Given the often-antagonistic attributes associated with an animal rights position, it is little wonder that critics would want to distance Costello from Coetzee. While none of these distancing strategies is particularly negative— for example, the fool in Attwell's analysis is not necessarily a doomed figure but instead takes risks and opens up the realm of possibility—they are in fact based on readings of Costello as woman. That distinction in and of itself need not be sexist; the reasons for that distinction, however, are undeniably tainted by Costello's status as both female and elderly, a "fleshy, white-haired lady" (16). As such, she serves as the embodiment of all that is least respected in academia, a space where a woman's perceived intelligence decreases exponentially as she ages, thereby marking the degeneration of her currency as surrogate daughter and imaginary lover—someone like Melanie in *Disgrace,* for example—within the academy. The result is the rather unself-conscious and resounding need for Coetzee proponents to constantly deconstruct Coetzee and extract him from Costello without doing much in the way of analyzing the character of Costello herself. Instead, we theorize about the role Costello plays with regard to Coetzee's ideas about realism and are overwhelmed with the underlying "truth" in analyses of *The Lives of Animals* that Costello's voice is not Coetzee's, that Costello, as Austin Briggs claims, is a "made up novelist . . . who recast *Ulysses*—which recast *The Odyssey*—as *The House on Eccles Street,* in which she made up a character called Molly Bloom—who, of course, Joyce made up" (11). Furthermore and despite the fact that we know that Coetzee is "a vegetarian who does not drink or smoke" (Susskind), we also know that he does not voice his ethics in public; in fact he voices very little in public except his fiction, and he evades seemingly all questions that attempt to get at the truth everyone else seems so eager to ascribe to his work.

For example, one can envision the squirming of both interviewer and interviewee when Coetzee says to Tony Morphet, "your questions again and again drive me into a position I don't want to occupy" (464). Such antics cause Briggs to claim that Coetzee is "in conversation, the third most impossible person I have encountered in a fairly long life" (following Marisol and Ezra Pound) (11). In a literary-critical context, if you respect Coetzee's evasiveness, you must concede that *The Lives of Animals* is not his argument about animal rights because Coetzee would not make such an argument; however, he would (we might be willing to admit) do some gender-bending linguistic acrobatics in order to tease out a discourse on the human ability for imagined identification. In a discussion about *The Lives of Animals* at a two-day colloquium called *J. M. Coetzee and the Ethics of Intellectual Practice* at the University of Warwick, such logic was very apparent in Dominic Head's claim that in teaching *The Lives of Animals,* he tries to get his students to discuss the role of the sympathetic imagination, but—wonder of wonders—they want to talk about animal rights. Graham Huggan, while stopping short of acknowledging the performative, gave a nod to the spoken nature of Coetzee's project: *The Lives of Animals,* he claims, *is* a public argument, delivered in a public forum by Coetzee himself, about animal rights. Michael Pollan, in his argument *against* animal rights, also conflates Coetzee and Costello, asking

> will history someday judge us as harshly as it judges the Germans who went about their ordinary lives in the shadow of Treblinka? Precisely that question was posed by J. M. Coetzee . . . in a lecture he delivered at Princeton; he answers in the affirmative. If animal rightists are right, "a crime of stupefying proportions" (*in Coetzee's words*) is going on around us everyday. (61, my emphasis)

Similarly, animal rights proponent Charles Patterson attributes to Coetzee this passage from *The Lives of Animals* at the beginning of the third chapter of his book *Eternal Treblinka:* "let me say openly: we are surrounded by an enterprise of degradation, cruelty, and killing. . . ." Therefore, the "me" is assumed to be Coetzee, but readers know that this passage is spoken by Elizabeth Costello. If one reads for the animal rights argument, then, Costello's words become Coetzee's, but in both cases—the critic or the animal rights philosopher—one thing is very apparent: Elizabeth Costello is absent from the debate. Michael Pollan's claim that her words are "Coetzee's words" erases the character of Elizabeth Costello from the text, as does David Attwell's claim that Costello is a surrogate for Coetzee. We are placed in another either/or dilemma—either this argument is Coetzee's or it is *not* Coetzee's—that denies the character of Elizabeth Costello the power of signification within Coetzee's text.

In reading the character of Elizabeth Costello, a familiar question arises, does Coetzee have it in him to be the woman, and more significantly, what does it mean to be the woman in the context of aged, feminist author, ex-colonial, and current vegetarian? Do we as critics have it in us to let Coetzee perform the woman, or do we call for Costello's position—or something like it—in Coetzee's own voice or in a voice that we can more easily and comfortably distinguish from Coetzee's? As I stated earlier, Coetzee is a vegetarian, and according to Derek Attridge, in a description of two lunches, one with Derrida "who talks to [him] about carnophallocentrism while eating with gusto a plate of steak tartare" ("Following") and a vegetarian lunch with

Coetzee at Princeton before his Tanner lectures, Coetzee lives that aspect of his ethical identity at least in his private life. Why mediate that position through a fictional woman? Voicing a woman through fiction, Coetzee again exposes the fallacious reasoning that there is any consistent notion of the "real," a claim that is further supported by the fact that Costello first rears her gray head in Coetzee's essay, "What is Realism?" Such a stance destabilizes binary oppositions and allows the seemingly subdued and evasive Coetzee some fictionally explored emotions and the freedom to rant via the character of Elizabeth Costello.

In *The Lives of Animals,* Coetzee foregrounds the content of Costello's lectures within the context of women's argumentative strategies—not only those of the empathetic Costello but also those of her philosophical daughter-in-law, Norma. These strategies are ultimately negotiated by Costello's somewhat patronizing son, John Bernard, who considers his mother's interest in animal rights a "hobby horse" (16). What is therefore enacted by Coetzee is a debate that takes place primarily between two women, a debate reluctantly mediated by the auspiciously named John, who "has no opinions one way or the other" (17) about animal rights and who wonders why his mother cannot just stay home and care for her cats (38). Through John, the man who refuses to voice a position, Coetzee writes himself into the text while he simultaneously uses the power of women's rhetorical strategies about animal rights, a largely dismissed debate, to overwhelm and silence his own potential argument. In many ways, it is safe way out, this kind of performance, allowing us to pick apart not only Costello's problematic animal rights thesis but also to denounce the mode of that argument as sentimental or hyperbolic.

Furthermore, both Norma and Elizabeth's argumentative strategies constitute emotional "rants" when interpreted by John and his colleagues as well as (more often than not) by Coetzee's critics. Norma reacts bodily, "sighs" and "snorts" (32), during Costello's primary argument in "The Philosophers and the Animals" that to claim that "the meat industry is ultimately devoted to life . . . is to ask the dead of Treblinka to excuse their killers because their body fat was needed to make soap" (22). Furthermore, Costello's response to the treatment of animals is also bodily and therefore sentimental, as expressed through the self-righteous vegetarianism she practices to "save [her] soul" (43) and through her breakdown at the end of the narrative. But because Costello is voiced by Coetzee through his authorship of her speeches and through his literal voicing when he read them at Princeton, the gendering of her position is problematized. Terms like "rant," "sentiment," and "emotion" cease to find stability within a dualistic paradigm; that

Costello is effectively written out of critical debate is illustrative of women's relative invisibility within the codification of philosophical argument. Costello presents an academically sanctioned argument, and as an oral presentation characterized by "acrimony, hostility, bitterness" (67), that argument serves to polarize her audience. Polarization, we want to tell her, is not the right strategy to employ in an argument, but such a claim returns us to some very binary thinking: either one provides a measured and well-reasoned philosophical commentary on the subject, or one is disqualified from the debate.

One of the strengths of Coetzee's text is that it does present the plight of the woman with strong ethical convictions: she runs the risk of being silenced not only by other men, but also by other women, especially if her convictions are marginal to the dominant set of acceptable standards, and especially by women who have privileged rationality over feeling as Norma has. As the narrator states, Norma "has never hesitated to tell [John] that his mother's . . . ethical relations with animals are jejune and sentimental" (17). Norma's willingness to embrace rationalist philosophy, to argue that "there is no position outside of reason where you can stand and lecture about reason and pass judgement on reason" (48), puts her at odds with Costello who has concluded after "seven decades of life experience" that "reason is neither the being of the universe nor the being of God" (23). Furthermore, the language of female madness and gender-specific inferiority pervades this text, with Norma doing most of the name-calling. She calls Elizabeth "confused" (36) and "naive" (47), her lectures "absurd" (67); she claims in response to John's assertion that his mother is sincere, "mad people are sincere" (67), and she asserts that Elizabeth's vegetarianism is mere food faddism, a "crazy scheme" (68). In conjunction, Elizabeth passively fights back, goading Norma by asking why the children are not eating with them despite the fact that "she knows the answer" (16). Positioned as he is between the two women and despite his lack of stance (he says "I have no insight into my motives and I couldn't care less" (67)), John is hardly a neutral player. His male privilege is the cause of Norma's gender-specific "bitterness" (17), because he finds a job when she is unable to do so, just as he is the reason his mother dislikes Norma, a point inherent in his realization that "his mother would have chosen not to like any woman he married" (17). Symbolically larger than one husband or one son, John comes to stand for the male indifference that blocks women's interactions and affection for one another; the animal rights argument, in turn, becomes the metaphysical space within which both women beg John to signify, to take a position within this debate about sentiment and logic, theory and activism.

By relaying the animal rights argument through the female characters of Elizabeth and Norma, Coetzee effectively does several things, all of which have very much to do with femininity and feminism per se. Through the persona of Costello, Coetzee performs femininity and enacts embodiment in ways that counteract the masculinized notion of intellectual production Eugene Dawn describes in *Dusklands* as "the capacity to breed out of our own head" (26), the negation of the body which is, according to Judith Butler, the domain of women, slaves, animals and children: it is, after all, David's body that responds to Lucy's rape through its aversion to the eating of meat. According to Butler, man is rhetorically constructed and constituted as a being that "is without childhood, is not a primate and so is relieved of the necessity of eating, defecating, living and dying; one who is not a slave, but always a property holder; one whose language remains originary and untranslatable. . . . a figure of disembodiment" (*Bodies* 49). The animal rights argument delivered by Costello is, at its core, about bodies after all, regardless of our human ability to prove or disprove the existence of intellect as distinct from or enmeshed with those bodies. Such a claim is in line with feminist performance theory of the kind exemplified by Butler, combining, as Elin Diamond claims, the "most pressing questions of theatrical representation: Who is speaking and who is listening? Whose body is in view and whose is not? What is being represented, how, and with what effects? Who or what is in control?" (ii). Through performance, Coetzee illustrates the potential plight of the female philosopher who uses empathy as well as logic in her argument. Especially in the realm of animal rights, a discourse always in danger of being trivialized or deemed sentimental in nature, the empathetic voice—male or female—may always run the risk of being feminized; if that voice is in fact a female voice, it runs the risk of being hystericalized as well. This voice is only treated in such a way, however, when underscored by John, the male player in this drama, whose apathy functions to silence the competing arguments of the two women in his life. In this context, the connections between animal rights and women's rights come to the forefront. Just as, according to Carol J. Adams, "animals are made absent through language that renames dead bodies before consumers participate in eating them" (42), the more emotional rhetorical stance of Costello is negated in favor of rationality, and Costello herself becomes the absent referent in discussions about Coetzee's project.

The connections between animal rights and women's rights, indeed between animal rights and human rights, have been very explicitly stated by feminist scholars who seek to destabilize the binary thinking that designates animals as different from humans within the realm of rights. The underlying ecofeminist theory in works like Marjorie Spiegel's *The Dreaded Comparison: Human and Animal Slavery*, Lori Gruen's "Dismantling Oppression: An Analysis of the Connection Between Women and Animals," and, as I have previously mentioned, Carol J. Adams's *The Sexual Politics of Meat: A Feminist-Vegetarian Critical Theory*, is holistic in nature: humans learn to "other" humans in their othering of animals. Animal rights philosopher Charles Patterson supports the feminist claim that "the sexual subjugation of women, as practiced in all the known civilizations of the world, was modeled on the domestication of animals" (12). To unlearn this primary binary opposition of animal/human is to begin to undo oppression from the ground up. But despite the fact that women very often do the manual and emotional labor within the animal rights movement (Gruen 81)—just as Bev Shaw is the person who euthanizes the animals in *Disgrace* while David disposes of their bodies—male philosophers like Tom Regan and Peter Singer, philosophers who privilege another either/or system of philosophical thought by advocating either an animal rights agenda based on natural rights theory or on utilitarianism, tend to get most of the credit. It is therefore worth noting that in critical debate about *The Lives of Animals*, the more rational aspects of the animal rights argument are attributed to Coetzee while the excitable speech inherent in the rant is attributed to Costello.

That a male voice reads Costello's problematic thesis, that the slaughter of animals in contemporary cultures is analogous to the Holocaust, pushes an already precariously balanced argument over the rhetorical precipice. The woman as conduit for such an argument marks such a comparison as excessive. Elizabeth Costello even admits to an excess of feeling, embracing the rhetoric that designates and negates her as hysterical, when she breaks down and cries to her son John at the end of the narrative: "I seem to move around perfectly easily among people, to have perfectly normal relations with them. Is it possible, I ask myself, that all of them are participants in a crime of stupefying proportions? Am I fantasizing it all? I must be mad!" (69). Yet Isaac Bashevis Singer made the same claim before Costello, and his statement from "The Writer," that "in relationship to them, all people are Nazis; for the animals, it is an eternal Treblinka," forms the title of Charles Patterson's 2002 release of *Eternal Treblinka: Our Treatment of Animals and the Holocaust*. It would seem that since this book is being heralded as perhaps the most important animal rights text since Peter Singer's *Animal Liberation* (Akers), the contentious Holocaust comparison is one whose time has come. But a look at the history of the animal rights movement in the United States and an examination of the plight of Elizabeth Costello makes clear the frustration that women have long experienced in the formulation of the kind of ethical philosophy for which Patterson is receiving so much praise. Very often, the female voice has been quieted, removed from the intellectual debate by the time that debate reaches a codified context, and what is considered radical when presented from a male perspective is often considered hysterical when it comes from a woman. The overarching complaint among the feminist animal rights theorists discussed in this chapter is with the pervasive acceptance of normative dualism within natural rights and utilitarian schools of thought, a binary paradigm that privileges reason over emotion, rational philosophy over rant.

In *The Lives of Animals,* Coetzee examines the way we treat our weakest while he demonstrates the ethical conflicts and at times apparent impossibilities of holistic thinking that subverts notions of genre, dualism, and linearity. Conversely, in their unwillingness to allow Coetzee a performative and feminist enactment of an ethical stance, his critics illustrate the limitations of the sympathetic imagination. By enacting Costello, Coetzee gets a rant and a sentimental voice presented through a rational argument, no matter how excessive any given audience may find that argument; he can illustrate the complexities of a lived ethical stance within the context of an intellectual presentation that runs up against literary and critical negotiations of the master narrative of philosophical debate. Costello's spoken animal rights argument within Coetzee's text is on the one hand about our treatment of animals, both human and nonhuman, but it is also a rhetorical exercise of the sympathetic imagination and the role that imagining plays in breaking down binary distinctions. His performance of Elizabeth Costello restores the absent referent to the narrative, but her invisibility as an entity worthy of critical debate points to the resilience of those dualistic categories, the difficulty of ethical human change through identification with other lives including the lives of animals. As Joy Williams claims:

> the animal people are calling for a moral attitude toward a great and mysterious mute nation. Their quest is quixotic; their reasoning assailable; their intentions, almost inarticulateable. The implementation of their wisdom would seem madness. But the future world is not this one. Our treatment of animals and our attitude toward them are crucial not only to any pretensions we have to ethical behavior but to humankind's intellectual and moral evolution. Which is how the human animal is meant to evolve, isn't it? (*Ill Nature* 177)

The mediating and logical voice of John asks Elizabeth, "do you really believe, Mother, that poetry classes are going to close down the slaughterhouses?" (58), and one could ask Coetzee the same question of his own literature, a question that he is perhaps asking of himself and of us when he performs the character of Elizabeth Costello, the embodied presence that not only rants but also acts through the medium of fiction.

My somewhat backwards way of approaching the character of Elizabeth Costello after an examination of *Disgrace* in this chapter is also a way of restoring her—perhaps even resurrecting her after the fact—to the text as Coetzee's critique of imagined identification as well as his embodiment of the mediating voice, the performative voice that Coetzee inhabits when he speaks Elizabeth Costello, the voice that is neither Coetzee's nor Costello's, neither male nor female, neither fully rational nor emotional. This is the voice that not only problematizes the dichotomous logic responsible for the binary oppositions of colonial and patriarchal thought, including the animal/human dualism, but that also disrupts the privileging of the rational over the emotional by calling into question assumptions about author, narrator, protagonist, text, and audience. The resounding but not at all negatively connoted "no" that serves as a response to the dialogic question as to whether David Lurie can "be" the woman is *Disgrace* is explicated, parodied, and ultimately elevated in *The Lives of Animals*. While one can never *be* the other, Coetzee's performance indicates, on an ethical level, one must continue to attempt to imagine the subjectivity of that which one is not. But more importantly, when we fail in that attempt—as we certainly will—we must continue to grant ethical consideration to that which cannot be imagined and to respect the alterity of those beings with whom we share, as Elizabeth Costello claims, the "substrate of life."

Conclusion

In her 1991 Nobel Lecture, "Writing and Being," Nadine Gordimer claims that "writers themselves don't analyze what they do; to analyze would be to look down while crossing a canyon on a tightrope." In his 2003 Nobel Lecture, "He and His Man," Coetzee looks down into the neverland of Gordimer's canyon. He speaks, as he most often does in such instances, through the fictional, telling a story rather than delivering a more standard lecture; this narrative is focalized through Robinson Crusoe as he ponders his relationship both to Friday and to Defoe's narrative of life on the island. All things and all narratives become, according to the third-person narrator, "a figure of the shipwreck and the island where he, poor Robin, was secluded from the world for 26 years," an auspicious number that also constitutes the length of time from the publication of *In the Heart of the Country* in 1977 to Coetzee's speech before the Nobel committee. This speech, like much of Coetzee's writing, is a metafictional exploration of imagined identification—Coetzee's identification with Crusoe (as imagined by Defoe) as Crusoe tries to imagine a relationship with Friday. And as is the case with many of Coetzee's third-person narrators, the narrative voice asks dialogic questions that place the audience in a position to answer: "how are they to be figured, this man and he? As master and slave? As brothers, twin brothers? As comrades in arms? Or as enemies, foes?"

Coetzee's writerly tendency, here as elsewhere, is to strip language of its metaphorical content and to reveal what lies beneath: the uninhabitable being of the other. While Gordimer, in "Writing and Being," situates herself as a writer in South Africa as the Kafkan dog "Nevermore"—the "mongrel Great Dane [with] an appearance that centuries of the most careful breeding could never have produced"—Coetzee dispels the metaphor of the dog, claiming that in a fever, Robinson imagines that "the devil lay upon him in his bed in the shape of a huge dog" only to realize days later that "neither dog nor devil had lain upon him." As Dostoevsky realizes in *The Master of Peters-burg,* the dog is not a sign, not evidence of god or the devil. The dog is (or in the case of Coetzee's lecture, the dog is *not*). The body of the other is not a sign, but an impenetrable body. Whether that body belongs to an animal, a black South African, or a member of another gender, it maintains a con-sciousness that may be mimicked or performed but never fully known. In his discussion of the alienation effect that I explicate earlier in this study, Brecht discusses the role of gender, claiming that "if the part is played by somebody of the opposite sex the sex of the character will be more clearly brought out" (192). Therefore, attempted identification on the part of the audience with the position of either a member of the opposite sex or an animal results in the audience's sense of alienation from, rather than identification with, the characters onstage. The same can be said of fiction in which authors con-struct characters who perform (characters who therefore attempt to imagine the interiority of) members of the opposite sex or who attempt to imagine an animal's consciousness. Such moments of alienation lead to a sense of destabilization that forces the audience to acknowledge not only difference, but also ethical responsibility for that which is different.

    With Brecht's analysis of drag and its relation to the alienation effect in mind, at the end of this study I want to return to Olive Schreiner's *The Story of an African Farm,* particularly the chapter entitled "Gregory's Woman-hood" and to read it through Coetzee's presentation of Elizabeth Costello's "apehood" in *The Lives of Animals,* both texts providing examples of male performance of a specific female subjectivity as well as an imagined animal consciousness—the two tenets upon which this study is based. In *The Story of an African Farm,* the character of Gregory decides to dress as a female nurse in order to serve the dying Lyndall. Prior to shaving his beard and don-ning women's clothing, Gregory asks of no one in particular—in what con-stitutes a dialogic moment within the text—"am I, am I Gregory Nazianzen Rose?" (238). The only entities within the text that hear this question are animals that are treated anthropomorphically, as conspirators in Gregory's performance of femininity. As he dresses in women's clothing, a meerkat "sat on her hind legs watching" (239), and ants carry away his beard trimmings to line their nests, removing all evidence of his masculinity. Lyndall's dog Doss watches Gregory enter the room and his "small head and bright eyes looked knowingly" (240) through Gregory's disguise. Gregory's performance as Lyndall's nurse functions in a twofold manner: first, he enacts a feminine position not only to care for Lyndall but also to be like her, and plays his part so well that the doctor claims s/he is the best nurse he has ever seen. Sec-ondly, and more significantly, Gregory, in the guise of a woman, can enact

Lyndall's absent lover, the unnamed "stranger" who exists "offstage" in this narrative. As he cares for her, Gregory caresses Lyndall, kisses her feet (248), and when she falls, "very softly Gregory's hands disrobed her" (250). As a woman, Gregory can parody the man he aspires to be in Lyndall's life; he is able to mimic if not perform the sexual ministrations of Lyndall's mysterious stranger.

While Schreiner's narrative stops short of Gregory's imagined identification with animals—animals, in fact, seem to imagine being human in *The Story of an African Farm*—Schreiner does place a male subjectivity within a female subject position. The character of Elizabeth Costello in many ways constitutes J. M. Coetzee's own imagined womanhood, the character that allows him to voice, through mimesis, views that otherwise might remain, like Lyndall's nameless lover, offstage. As I have already discussed, Costello is the persona to whom Coetzee ascribes an entire body of philosophical speeches that he himself delivers before various audiences, thereby performing Costello's rhetoric and ideology, however similar or different they may be from his own, and Costello asks a dialogic question that mirrors Gregory's in terms of the limits of imagined identification. After she discusses her ability, as a writer, to imagine herself as dead, Elizabeth Costello asks, "if we are capable of thinking our own death, why on earth should we not be capable of thinking our way into the life of a bat?" (33). The various audiences that inhabit and that exist external to *The Lives of Animals* may attempt to answer, but the question will always remain, indicative of the interregnum between a failure of the sympathetic imagination and the potential for ethical action in spite of that failure.

In *The Lives of Animals,* Costello claims that

> it is two years since I last spoke in the United States. In the lecture I then gave, I had reason to refer to the great fabulist Franz Kafka, and in particular to his story about an educated ape. . . . On that occasion I felt a little like Red Peter myself and said so. Today that feeling is even stronger. (18)

Costello—or Coetzee via Costello, it is hard to tell which—refers to Kafka's "Report to an Academy," a story about Red Peter, "Kafka's . . . ape who performs" (18). The ape to whom Costello claims allegiance is anthropomorphically rendered, another being in drag who dresses in human clothing and speaks human words. But the lives of animals she discusses in her lectures, and the lives of animals that Coetzee depicts in his novels, are animals who cannot speak, who must rely on human ability to engage in a dialogue of imagined identification with them; they are animals headed for the abattoir or the pound. In spite of her assertion that she is able to think her way into the consciousness of such animals, whether Costello (or Coetzee via Costello) does successfully imagine this subjectivity is unlikely: in the context of South Africa, as Coetzee has claimed, the body takes precedence, and the animal body as that which cannot be voiced, performed, or usurped, is the ideal stabilizer of Coetzee's interregnum narratives, the body that is situated between one dying order and the unspeakable unforeseen paradigm that will replace it.

Coetzee teases out my aforementioned discourse of the parodic nature of the performative in the final lesson of *Elizabeth Costello*, "The Gate," a narrative in which Costello finds herself in a purgatory of sorts, a self-conscious Kafkaesque "literary theme park" (208) (as the narrator claims, "Kafka reduced and flattened to a parody" (209)) within which she examines and critiques the obviousness of the performance that takes place all around her, asking "why is the make-up so poor? Why is the whole thing not done better?" (208). Coetzee's awareness of the parody that he enacts when he performs Elizabeth Costello is brought to the forefront; Costello's admission that "I do not give shows . . . I'm not an entertainer" (214) became resoundingly ironic as Coetzee stood before his audience at the University of Massachusetts performing what I tend to call "The Elizabeth Costello Show." Coetzee and Costello speak to one another, engage in dialogue before an audience. As Judith Shulevitz asserts in her *New York Times Book Review* of *Elizabeth Costello*, "perhaps the way to look at Costello is as just one player in a series of narratives that in their very sparseness achieve the dramatic tension of philosophical dialogues" (15). And in her realization that there exists a "gap between the actors and the parts they play" (209), Elizabeth Costello seems to voice Coetzee, to answer all the critics who want to distance him from or conflate him with the character of this female persona.

It is, this interstitial voice seems to tell us, only the "play" in which the writer can believe. Play—as both a theatrical performance and as participation in a writerly game—continues to characterize Coetzee's post-Nobel Prize opus: Elizabeth Costello first gets her own novel and later appears in *Slow Man* (2005) encouraging protagonist Paul Raymant (a character who claims early in the novel, "I am not Robinson Crusoe" (14)) to signify differently within the text, to "make a stronger case for [him]self" (82). Coetzee's writing reveals the often humorous, transparent beauty of the imagination at work, forever trying to place itself within the consciousness of the other. This subjectivity, in its various incarnations as David Lurie, Elizabeth Curren, Fyodor Dostoevsky, or Coetzee's other focalizing characters, constantly seeks common ground with the other and is somehow always humbled to find itself, instead, on the outside looking in, performing an identity that it can never become. This performance, this play, according to Costello, is what matters, "even if it is only a simulacrum" (*Elizabeth Costello* 215).

Afterword

At the Gate

October 23, 2003, the day after I hear him read from *Elizabeth Costello,* I think that J. M. Coetzee writes allegories about allegories. Or even more specifically, Coetzee writes allegories about the writing of allegories, a kind of meta-meta-fiction that should, by all logic, ring hollow at such a far remove from "the truth." But, of course, it doesn't ring hollow at all, and the "real" that is cast back through the fiction becomes the reflection, the simulacrum, the thing beyond the gate that, while bright, is not unimaginable at all.

The day before, however, I was too nervous to think. I managed to get out of bed and then wondered for approximately one entire hour what one wears when one meets J. M. Coetzee at the airport—if one is me, that is. It's all about the context of the thing, really. You or someone like you might wear jeans or you might wear something more formal. I, on the other hand, might need to look professional, or I might not. I'm never quite sure. So I compromise and wear brown pants and a black sweater, fake leather shoes, and I drive my car with its fake cow skin seat covers to the airport. There are degrees of parody in my accoutrements, just as—as Stephen Clingman has suggested to me—there are degrees of violence in Coetzee's fiction. The shoes on my feet look like leather but feel like rubber; my feet sweat and steam. The cow covers, on the other hand, look like cartoon cows, a print on furry fabric. Such mockery of animal flesh, I think, might not be lost on Coetzee.

But then again I worry about the overstatement that I may make with the car, that green 1998 VW Beetle with the cow seat covers, the vegan bumper sticker, and me in my purple, fake suede jacket. The car is at once performance and necessity, the way I take myself to meet Coetzee, and also the thing that makes a superficial statement about my beliefs and presents me as all together contradictory: can one be a vegan and drive a car that burns fossil fuel, the product of decaying animal matter? Am I, with my several

127

published articles about his work, my book about his dogs and his female narrators, a parody of an academic expert on Coetzee, a man I've never met? Am I a woman performing the role of the critic, or a woman performing the role of a woman about to meet a man, a woman checking her hair, wanting to be pretty, worried about her outfit? Or am I both?

At the airport, I pace because when I try to sit down, I have trouble breathing. My insides are in turmoil; I keep thinking that I might have to duck into the bathroom and throw up. I'm sweating even though it's cold enough to snow. I am always confounded by the influence of my mind on my body, and vice versa. I wait. Check the flight arrival screen. His flight from Chicago is on time, and I'm suddenly filled with dread, suddenly wishing I had more time, that there had been a delay. I have granted this man all manner of attributes, have established a whole system of belief about him based on nothing more (or nothing less?) than his words. In the interregnum between my idea of him and the performance that he will enact when I meet him, I go over, yet again, the conversations that I imagine we might have and try to test out all of the possible outcomes. Will he remain somber-faced and refuse to speak? Will I say the wrong thing and offend him? Will I look like a fool? The screen says that his flight has landed. I keep pacing, look fixedly toward the gate from which he will emerge, that gate that I cannot approach because of all the possible terrorists or barbarians and our national fear of their impending arrival.

And then there he is, coming towards me through that gate, not seeing me, not knowing me or having any need to know me. I, on the other hand, know him instantly and am taken momentarily aback by how familiar he seems, a body present before me, no longer a photographic representation. I am watching him and he is not watching me; I think that he is slight, nicely dressed, younger looking than I had imagined. I notice that his head is cocked ever so slightly to the left. He's alone, the light behind him coming through the full-length window, making him almost a silhouette. And I think that this man, walking somewhat uncertainly, is J. M. Coetzee. And I wave, catch his eye, change the course of his trajectory. I wonder again, in that moment before he reaches me, who he really is and what I'm to call him: Dr.? Mr.? Professor? Is there, just inside his outside, the slightest outline of an elderly woman, white-haired, Australian?

Then he's there and he smiles—a surprise! In all the pictures on book jackets and in newspapers, I've never seen him smile; he is forever staring forward or caught mid-sentence behind a podium. For a moment I am filled with doubt, afraid to trust either one of us not to turn to mist and fade. I may have said hello. Perhaps I smiled back. He extends a hand.

"I'm Laura," I say.

"Hello, Laura. I'm John," he replies.

Notes

1. According to Dorothy Driver, for *Drum*'s male writers, "the magazine offered a vehicle that was part training ground and part enabling community. It offered quite the reverse for women. Only two black South African women published books written in English in the 1960s—Noni Jabavu and Bessie Head—and both did so from outside the country" (231).

2. Both novels are concerned with representations of historical truth, Gordimer's with the repression of indigenous South African suffering characterized by the black body that keeps surfacing on the white farmer Mehring's farm and Head's with the chronicling of mental illness and its associations with miscegenation: "We have a full docket on you. You must be very careful. Your mother was insane. If you're not careful you'll get insane just like your mother. Your mother was a white woman. They had to lock her up, as she was having a child by the stable boy, who was a native" (16).

3. Purkey admitted his own artistic difficulties during a two-part graduate/faculty seminar, hosted by the Interdisciplinary Seminar in the Humanities and Fine Arts (ISHA), University of Massachusetts-Amherst, on April 12, 2001.

4. See Laura Wright, "Minor Literature and 'The Skeleton of Sense': Anorexia, Franz Kafka's 'A Hunger Artist,' and J. M. Coetzee's *Life and Times of Michael K*" in *The Journal of Commonwealth and Postcolonial Studies* 8.1 (2001): 109–123.

5. The concept of minor literature depends entirely on the existence of a major literature or established literary canon within the major language tradition of the minor author. According to David Lloyd, major literature "represents the common properties, the essential passions, of human beings, implying the universality of the forms of human nature" (20). A second necessary condition for minor literature is that everything in the work is political, whereas in major literature, the individual is highlighted against the back-

ground of the social environment. The third and final criterion of minor literature is that everything in the text takes on collective value. Because collective national or cultural consciousness is inactive in real or external life and is "always in the process of breakdown" (Deleuze and Guattari 17), minor literature becomes an agent of collective and revolutionary enunciation.

6. Nadine Gordimer uses this quote from Gramsci as the epigraph to *July's People*. In a note in Gordimer's essay, "Living in the Interregnum," Stephen Clingman notes that the quote appears in a slightly different translation in *Selections from the Prison Notebooks of Antonio Gramsci;* ed. and trans. by Quintin Hoare and Geoffrey Nowell Smith (London: Lawrence & Wishart, 1971).

7. The concept of the "floating signifier" appears first as an "empty signifier" in Roland Barthes's essay "Myth Today," cited below from *Mythology;* translated by Annette Lavers (New York: Hill and Wang, 1997). Barthes says that "the signifier of myth presents itself in an ambiguous way: it is at the same time meaning and form, full on one side and empty on the other . . . when it becomes form, the meaning leaves its contingency behind; it empties itself, it becomes impoverished, history evaporates, only the letter remains" (117).

8. Both Gordimer's *July's People* (1981) and Coetzee's *Life & Times of Michael K* (1983) present an apocalyptic vision of a possible future and have been critically compared to one another. When Tony Morphet asked Coetzee about critical comparisons, Coetzee responded, "fortunately Michael K had been born and was living his own life by the time I read *July's People,* so I didn't have to worry about questions of influence. . . . I don't recognize important similarities between the books" (458).

9. According to Ashcroft, Griffiths, and Tiffin in *Key Concepts in Post-Colonial Studies,* "allegory has long been a prominent feature in literary and mythic writing throughout the world, but it becomes particularly significant for post-colonial writers for the way in which it disrupts notions of orthodox history, classical realism and imperial representation in general"(9). Furthermore, Fredric Jameson made a controversial suggestion with regard to allegory in "Third World Literature in the era of Multi-national Capitalism:" "Third World texts . . . necessarily project a political dimension in the form of national allegory; the story of the private individual destiny is always an allegory of the embattled situation of the public third world culture and society" (88).

10. Furthermore, Coetzee further links the dialogic with the radical: "what's missing in Bahktin, [is] namely, a clear statement that dialogism as exemplified in the novels of Dostoevsky is a matter not of ideological position, still less of novelistic technique, but the most radical intellectual and even spiritual courage" (*Stranger Shores* 123).

11. Adams discusses the absent referent specifically within the context of the language used to characterize meat as distinct from animals: "through butchering, animals become absent referents. Animals in name and body are made absent *as animals* for meat to exist" (40).

12. One of the most famous literary depictions of the impossibility of reciprocity between colonizer and colonized takes place at the end of E. M. Forster's *A Passage to India.* Fielding questions why he and Dr. Aziz cannot be friends "now"—in the present, an instant during which the colonial framework is fully in place—as opposed to after the English are driven from India in some unknowable future moment. His answer comes not from Aziz, but from the landscape:

> the horses didn't want it—they swerved apart; the earth didn't want it . . . the temples, the tank, the jail, the palace, the birds, the carrion, the Guest House . . : they didn't want it, they said in their hundred voices, "No, not yet," and the sky said, "No, not there." (362)

In *A Passage to India,* the laboring animals—the horses beneath their human riders—and the land beneath the horses' hooves establish a hierarchy that extends upwards to include the dualism of self and other inherent in the colonial relationship between the English Fielding and the Indian Aziz. Furthermore, the human-made symbols of religion and empire—the temples, the jail, the palace—stand incongruously beside one another, unable to reconcile their existence with the absolute alterity of the non-human world represented by the birds above and the dead below. In the interregnum depicted in Forster's India, binary oppositions step to the forefront, bookending the historical moment of betweeness, illuminated beneath an unyielding sky, forced further apart by rocks jutting from a seemingly divisive earth. In the mythical "now" of the interregnum, the "voices" that resonate the loudest are not those of extant humanity; they are instead entities that must signify through the very absence of vocalization: the dead, the landscape, and as other silent but living beings, animals.

NOTES TO CHAPTER TWO

1. See, for example, North American author John Edgar Wideman's *The Cattle Killing.*

2. I have chosen to highlight the Xhosa cattle killing because of its sheer magnitude, both in terms of its literary reverberations and its historical significance. The killing, however, is a specific event that was perpetuated by a specific indigenous South African population, the Xhosa. It should not, therefore, be read as a sweeping statement—metaphorical or historical—of the role of the animal in other indigenous South African cultures, despite its

relevance as an historical marker and its frequency, which is not at all surprising given the magnitude of the event, as a literary trope.

3. In contemporary ethnic American literature, for example, the animal metaphor is used very explicitly to illustrate the plight of various historical groups of people with a putatively common history. In Toni Morrison's *Beloved*, for example, Schoolteacher compares the slaves to animals as he attempts to justify slaveholding through rational empiricism. According to Ellen J. Goldner, initially, "Sethe describes the measuring of her nose and backsides in their early encounters as 'foolishness'" (77), but the outcome of such a comparison proves to be anything but laughable. As a result of the lessons Schoolteacher teaches his nephews, lessons that require the listing of Sethe's animal characteristics alongside her human attributes (193), the nephews steal Sethe's milk in a brutal act of rape. After Sethe admits to Paul D. that she attempts to kill her four children to keep them from having to return with Schoolteacher to Sweet Home, he says, "you got two feet, Sethe, not four" (165), an accusation that, while it ostensibly negates Sethe's status as animal, also reinforces the comparison. In Morrison's narrative, the institution of slavery turns everyone into animals; the self-fulfilling prophecy of Schoolteacher's comparison causes Sethe to behave like an animal just as Schoolteacher "increasingly appears as the emblem of all that is most Other to the human life of the slave" (Goldner 77). Despite the use of this comparative strategy, Morrison's narrative falls short of critiquing the foundational ideology that makes it impossible for humans to think of other animals as anything but directly oppositional.

    Furthermore, in Art Spiegelman's graphic novel *Maus*, Holocaust era Jews are depicted as mice, while Nazis are depicted as cats, Poles as pigs, and Americans as dogs. While such visual distinctions make manifest the predatory nature of the Nazis who sought to eliminate people they viewed as vermin (and subsequently killed with the rat poison Zyclon B), such differentiation is problematic because, by depicting groups of humans as different species of animals, Spiegelman in one sense highlights differences and separates certain groups of individuals—all of whom, we must concede, are human—from others. Sheng-Mei Ma questions the visual animal metaphor as well as Spiegelman's of pig masks worn by mice to pass as Poles:

    > Is ethnicity then, like a mask, a manufactured artifact, molded in part from some ethnic pain? Or is it the face? Is it the space between the face and the mask? Which one is the face and which the mask? Are there multiple masks or multiple faces? In *Maus*, do human beings wear animal masks or do animals wear human masks? (120)

4. Schreiner's novel is, according to Coetzee, anti-pastoral, written against the Afrikaans *plaasroman* or farm novel tradition that romanticized farm life.

Coetzee reads *Story of an African Farm* as "a figure in the service of [Schreiner's] critique of colonial culture" (*White Writing* 66).

5. In Schreiner's own feminist and anti-colonial life as well as in her art, the silent enunciators of child and animal define the nature of interregnum relationships: before she died, Schreiner requested that her own daughter, a baby that lived a mere sixteen days, and her favorite dog, Nita, were to be buried with her (First and Scott 254).

6. As the reception of Harriet Beecher Stowe's *Uncle Tom's Cabin* and its impact on the abolitionist movement in the United States illustrated. Furthermore, within the realm of environmental history, Rachel Carson's *Silent Spring* (1962) "linked traditional wildlife protection issues with urban-industrial ones" by evoking the sentimental, "the deathlike silence of a small-town spring once heralded by a chorus of birdsong" (Beinart and Coates 95).

7. This portrait appears in Burt Britton's *Self-Portraits: Book People Picture Themselves* (New York: Random House, 1976).

8. This mentality is still firmly in place in the minds of the modern-day safari-goers who, according to Joy Williams, want to maintain the illusion "that wild animals exist" since in many ways, postcolonial Africa is "a sad landscape, scorched, dispirited, full of people and cattle. Cattle and people are just cattle and people, after all" ("Safariland" 27). Inherent if not explicit in such thinking is the premise that one may still control what one sees just as Jacobus controls and orders by killing. Destruction of the landscape and its inhabitants has been replaced by the ordering of the visual South African narrative: now the camera acts as the gun once did. Such a mentality not only perpetuates the dualistic thinking that designates animals as other but also extends that thinking to privilege specific animals over others in the realm of the visual, the wild over the domestic. The fetishization of endangered species invokes a colonial history that has eradicated specific animals—and people—in the quest for control the landscape. Cattle and people are simply cattle and people, and the two categories of being are granted the same degree of humanity in Jacobus's narrative.

9. This myth can be undermined by a look at the historical record. Richard Leaky and Roger Lewin, for example, explain the history of the earth as if it were contained in a 1000 page book. According to Patterson,

> If each page covers four and a half million years, it would take 750 pages just to reach the beginnings of life in the sea. Hominids would not appear until three pages from the end of the book . . . . The story of Homo sapiens would be told in the very last line of the book, with everything from cave paintings and the pyramids to the Holocaust and computer age jammed into the final word. (4)

10. Derek Attridge quotes Derrida's definition of the *arrivant* in *Aporias*: "this word can . . . mean the neutrality of that which arrives, but also the singularity of who arrives, he or she who comes, coming to be where he or she was not expected" ("Expecting" 27).

11. For example, in *Life & Times of Michael K*, after his mother's death, Michael scatters her ashes, "closes his eyes and concentrated hoping that a voice would speak reassuring him that what he was doing was right . . . . But no voice came" (58). In the interregnum, the body (or its ashes) must signify for itself as must the earth to which Michael commits it. Ultimately, Michael forgoes his quest for signs opting instead to care for the land for the sake of the land. Conversely, when Susan Barton arrives on Cruso's island in *Foe*, she senses the rocking of the island as a "sign [she is] becoming an island dweller" (26), and later, when an unfamiliar girl appears claiming to be her daughter, Susan wonders "what is she a sign of?" (79). Susan seeks signs the entire novel, and as a result, is unable to grant alterity to the silent Friday who gives her no signs, provides her with no narrative to explain his voicelessness.

12. See, for example, Coetzee's review of Joseph Frank's biography of Dostoevsky, *The Miraculous Years* (in *Stranger Shores*, 114-126) as well as "Confession and Double Thoughts: Tolstoy, Rousseau, Dostoevsky" (in *Doubling the Point* 251-293).

13. And there is further evidence within the text to support a reading of both Nechaev and Pavel as homosexual, including Dostoevsky's reference to Nechaev in drag as part of "Pavel's erotic surround" (98) and his later statement to Nechaev that "'I wish I could have heard you and Pavel together.' What he does not say is: Like two swords, two naked swords" (195).

NOTES TO CHAPTER FOUR

1. Again I am referencing Scarry here in her discussion of the role of interrogation in terms of torture. She claims that while "the information sought in an interrogation is almost never credited with being a *just* motive for torture, it is repeatedly credited with being the motive for torture." Furthermore, "as the content and context of the torturer's questions make clear, the fact that something is asked *as if* the content of the answer matters does not mean that it matters. It is crucial to see that the interrogation does not stand outside an episode of torture as its motive or justification: it is internal to the structure of torture, exists there because of its intimate connections to and interactions with the physical pain" (28–29).

2. The only potential reference to Michael's race is written on a charge sheet after he is arrested: "Michael Visagie—CM—40—NFA—Unemployed" (70) with "CM" possibly standing for "colored male." Given that we know

that Visagie is not Michael's name, and given that we know his age to be 31 and not 40, we must read "CM" as an equally untrustworthy distinction.

3. For a much more detailed discussion of the role of ritual in both torture and war, see Michel Foucault's *Discipline and Punish* discussion of "torture [as] technique" (33) and public execution "not only as a judicial, but also a political ritual" (47).

NOTES TO CHAPTER FIVE

1. See in particular Derek Attridge, "Age of Bronze, State of Grace: Music and Dogs in Coetzee's *Disgrace." Novel: A Forum on Fiction* 34.1(2000): 98–121, and Lucy Graham, "'Yes, I am giving him up': Sacrificial Responsibility and Likeness with Dogs in J. M. Coetzee's Recent Fiction." *Scrutiny2: Issues in English Studies in Southern Africa* 7.1(2000): 4–15.

2. According to Cecilia Conway, "in the twentieth century the banjo thrives in the upland South[ern United States] and is an emblem of white mountain folk; but this has not always been so. Blacks brought the banjo to this country from Africa, and the instrument remained with them for many years" (135).

3. The narrative is filled with references to guides of various kinds. David apologizes to Lucy for "not turning out to be a better guide" (79) and thinks of her again later as the daughter "whom it has fallen to [him] to guide. Who one day will guide [him]" (156). Lucy rebuffs David's actions in this capacity claiming, "you are not the guide I need, not at this time" (161). Bev claims to be an "escort" (84) for the animals she ushers into the after-life. The narrative voice also asks of David, "if he is being led, then what god is doing the leading?" (192).

4. Not incidentally, when Flaubert was brought to court on charges of obscenity and asked to identify the "real" Madame Bovary, he made the now famous claim, "Madame Bovary, c'est moi." Such a statement, as both the author's claim of imagined identification with the woman and simultaneous refusal of some expected confession, is certainly not lost on Coetzee with regard to David Lurie.

Bibliography

Adams, Carol J. *The Sexual Politics of Meat: A Feminist-Vegetarian Critical Theory.* New York: Continuum, 1996.

Adelman, Gary. "Staking Stavrogin: J. M. Coetzee's *The Master of Petersburg* and the Writing of the Possessed." *Journal of Modern Literature* 23.2 (1999–2000): 351–56.

Akers, Keith. "Asking the Big Questions." Rev. of *Eternal Treblinka: Our Treatment of Animals and the Holocaust,* by Charles Patterson. *Compassionate Spirit* 11 Dec. 2005. <http://www.compassionatespirit.com/Eterna-Treblinka-review.html>

"An Interview with J. M. Coetzee." *World Literature Today* 70.1 (1996): 107–110.

Ascui, Francisco. "Multiculturalism." *Siglo2* Mar. 1994. <http://www.utas.edu.au/docs/siglo/mag/intro2.html>.

Ashcroft, Bill, Gareth Griffiths, and Helen Tiffin. *Key Concepts in Post-Colonial Studies.* London: Routledge, 1998.

Attridge, Derek. "Age of Bronze, State of Grace: Music and Dogs in Coetzee's *Disgrace.*" *Novel: A Forum on Fiction* 34.1(2000): 98–121.

———. "Expecting the Unexpected in Coetzee's *Master of Petersburg* and Derrida's Recent Writings." *Applying: to Derrida.* Ed. John Brannigan, Ruth Robbins, and Julian Wolfreys. New York: St. Martins, 1996. 21–40.

———. "Following Derrida." *Tympanum* 4 (2000). 17 Mar. 2003 <http://www.usc.edu/dept/comp-lit/tympanum/4/attridge.html>.

———. *J. M. Coetzee and the Ethics of Reading: Literature in the Event.* Chicago: U of Chicago P, 2004.

———. "J. M. Coetzee's *Boyhood,* Confession, Truth." *Critical Survey* 11.2 (1999): 77–93.

———. "Oppressive Silence: J. M. Coetzee's *Foe* and the Politics of the Canon." *Decolonizing Tradition: New Views of Twentieth-Century "British" Literary Canons.* Ed. Karen R. Lawrence. Urbana: U of Illinois P, 1992. 212–238.

———. "Trusting the Other: Ethics and Politics in J. M. Coetzee's *Age of Iron.*" *South Atlantic Quarterly* 93.1 (1994): 59–82.

Attwell, David. *J. M. Coetzee: South Africa and the Politics of Writing.* Berkeley: U of California P, 1993.

————. "The Lives and Times of Elizabeth Costello." Public Lecture. *J. M. Coetzee and the Ethics of Intellectual Practice: An International Conference.* University of Warwick, Coventry. 27 Apr. 2002.

Atwood, Margaret. *Surfacing.* New York: Simon and Schuster, 1972.

Azoulay, Ariella. "An Alien Woman/A Permitted Woman: On J. M. Coetzee's *Disgrace.*" *Scrutiny2: Issues in English Studies in Southern Africa* 7.1(2000): 33–41.

Backscheider, Paula R. and John J. Richetti, eds. *Popular Fiction by Women 1660–1730: An Anthology.* Oxford, Clarendon Press, 1996.

Bahktin, Mikhail. *The Dialogic Imagination: Four Essays.* Trans. Caryl Emerson and Michael Holquist. Ed. Michael Holquist. Austin: U of Texas P, 1981.

Barker, Francis, Peter Hulme, and Margaret Iversen, eds. *Cannibalism and the Colonial World.* Cambridge: Cambridge UP, 1998.

Barton, Judy L. "Coetzee's *Foe:* Humanitarianism in the Interregnum." *In-Between: Essays & Studies in Literary Criticism* 2.1 (1993): 37–43.

Begman, Richard. "Silence and Mut(e)ilation: White Writing in J. M. Coetzee's *Foe.*" *South Atlantic Quarterly* 93.1 (1994): 111–129.

Behdad, Ali. "Eroticism, Colonialism, and Violence." *Violence, Identity, and Self-Determination.* Ed. Hent de Vries. Stanford: Stanford UP, 1997. 201–207.

Beinart, William and Peter Coates. *Environment and History: The Taming of Nature in the USA and South Africa.* London: Routledge, 1995.

Bell, Michael. "What is it Like to be a Non-Racist?" Unpublished Conference Paper. *J. M. Coetzee and the Ethics of Intellectual Practice: An International Conference.* University of Warwick, Coventry. 27 Apr. 2002.

Bender, John. *Imagining the Penitentiary: Fiction and the Architecture of Mind in Eighteenth-Century England.* Chicago: U of Chicago P, 1987.

Bensmaia, Réda. "On the Concept of Minor Literature: From Kafka to Kateb Yacine." *Gilles Deleuze and the Theater of Philosophy.* Ed. Constantin V. Boundas and Dorothea Olkowski. New York: Routledge, 1994. 213–228.

Bethlehem, Louise. "Pliant/Compliant; Grace/*Disgrace;* Pliant/Compliant." *Scrutiny2: Issues in English Studies in Southern Africa* 7.1(2000): 20–24.

Biko, Steve. *I Write What I Like.* London: Bowerdean, 1996.

Boehmer, Elleke. "Sorry, Sorrier, Sorriest: The Gendering of Contrition in Coetzee's *Disgrace.*" Unpublished Conference Paper. *J. M. Coetzee and the Ethics of Intellectual Practice: An International Conference.* University of Warwick, Coventry. 27 April 2002.

Bower, Colin. "J. M. Coetzee: Literary Con Artist and Poseur." *Scrutiny2: Issues in English Studies in Southern Africa* 8.2 (2003): 3–23.

Brecht, Bertolt. *Brecht on Theatre.* Ed. and trans. John Willett. New York: Hill & Wang, 1964.

Briault-Manus, Vicki. "*In the Heart of the Country:* A Voice in a Vacuum." *Commonwealth Essays and Studies* 19.1 (1996): 60–70.

————. "The Colonialist Subject in 'The Narrative of Jacobus Coetzee' by J. M. Coetzee." *Commonwealth Essays and Studies* 18.1 (1995): 42–47.

Briganti, Chiara. "A Bored Spinster with a Locked Diary: The Politics of Hysteria in *In the Heart of the Country.*" *Research in African Literatures* 25.4 (1994): 33–49.

Briggs, Austin. "Who's Who When Everybody's at Home: James Joyce/J. M. Coetzee/Elizabeth Costello." *James Joyce Literary Supplement* 16.1 (2002): 11.

Brumberg, Joan Jacobs. *Fasting Girls: The History of Anorexia Nervosa.* New York: Vintage, 2000.

Butler, Anthony. *Democracy and Apartheid: Political Theory, Comparative Politics and the Modern South African State.* New York: St. Martin's, 1998.

Butler, Judith. *Bodies that Matter: On the Discursive Limits of "Sex."* New York: Routledge, 1993.

———. *Excitable Speech: A Politics of the Performative.* New York: Routledge, 1997.

Chernin, Kim. *The Hungry Self.* New York: Harper and Row, 1985.

Christman, Laura. *Rereading the Imperial Romance: British Imperialism and South African Resistance in Haggard, Schreiner, and Plaatje.* Oxford: Clarendon, 2000.

Cixous, Hélène. "The Laugh of the Medusa." *Feminisms: An Anthology of Literary Theory and Criticism.* Ed. Robyn R. Warhol and Diane Price Herndl. New Brunswick: Rutgers UP, 1993. 334–349.

Clingman, Stephen. "Nadine Gordimer: A Writing Life." *A Writing Life: Celebrating Nadine Gordimer.* Ed. Andries Walter Oliphant. London: Viking, 1998. 3–18.

———. *The Novels of Nadine Gordimer: History From the Inside.* London: Allen & Unwin, 1986.

———. "Surviving Murder: Oscillation and Triangulation in Nadine Gordimer's *The House Gun.*" *Modern Fiction Studies* 46.1 (2000): 139–158.

Coetzee, J. M. *Age of Iron.* New York: Penguin, 1990.

———. *Boyhood.* New York: Penguin, 1997.

———. "Confession and Double Thoughts: Tolstoy, Rousseau, Dostoevsky." *Doubling the Point.* Ed. David Attwell. Cambridge: Harvard UP, 1992. 251–293.

———. *Disgrace.* New York: Penguin, 1999.

———. *Doubling the Point.* Ed. David Attwell. Cambridge: Harvard UP, 1992.

———. *Dusklands.* New York: Penguin, 1985.

———. *Elizabeth Costello.* New York: Viking, 2003.

———. "Elizabeth Costello and the Problem of Evil." *Salmagundi* 137–138 (2003): 49–64.

———. *Foe.* New York: Penguin, 1986.

———. "He and His Man." Nobel Prize Lecture. *Nobel e-Museum.* 7 Dec. 2003. 23 Feb. 2004. <http://www.nobel.se/literature/laureates/2003/coetzee-lecture-e.html>.

———. *In the Heart of the Country.* New York: Penguin, 1982.

———. *Life & Times of Michael K.* New York: Penguin, 1985.

———. *The Lives of Animals.* Princeton: Princeton UP, 1999.

———. *The Master of Petersburg.* New York: Penguin, 1994.

———. "The Novel in Africa." *Occasional Papers of the Doreen B. Townsend Center for the Humanities,* no. 17, 1999.

———. *Slow Man.* New York: Viking, 2005.

————. *Stranger Shores: Literary Essays, 1986–1999*. New York: Viking, 2001.

————. *Waiting for the Barbarians*. New York: Penguin, 1980.

————. "What is Realism?" *Salmagundi* 114–15 (1997): 60–81.

————. *White Writing: On the Culture of Letters in South Africa*. New Haven: Yale UP, 1988.

————. *Youth*. New York: Penguin, 2003.

Collingwood-Whittick, Sheila. "J. M. Coetzee's *Dusklands:* Colonialist Myth as History." *Commonwealth Essays and Studies* 18.2 (1996): 75–89.

————. "In the Shadow of Last Things: The Voice of the Confessant in J. M. Coetzee's *Age of Iron*." *Commonwealth Essays and Studies* 19.1 (1996): 43–59.

————. "Writing by Numbers: Metafictional Musings on the Creative Process in *In the Heart of the Country*." *Commonwealth Essays and Studies* 22.1 (1999): 15–28.

Conquergood, Dwight. "Ethnography, Rhetoric, and Performance." *Quarterly Journal of Speech* 78 (1992): 80–123.

Conway, Cecilia. "The Banjo-Song Genre: A Study of 'High Sheriff,' Dink Roberts's Man-against-the-Law Song." *Arts in Earnest: North Carolina Folklife*. Ed. Daniel W. Patterson and Charles G. Zug III. Durham: Duke UP, 1990. 135–146.

Daymond, M. J. *South African Feminisms: Writing, Theory, and Criticism, 1990–1994*. New York: Garland, 1996.

de Jong, Marianna. "A Politics or an Ethics of Writing?" *Journal of Literary Studies/Tydskrif vir Literatuurwetenskap* 10.2 (1994): 227–237.

Deleuze, Gilles and Félix Guattari. *Kafka: Toward a Minor Literature*. Minneapolis: U of Minnesota P, 1986.

Diamond, Elin. *Unmaking Mimesis: Essays on Feminism and Theater*. London: Routledge, 1997.

Dodd, Josephine. "The South African Literary Establishment and the Textual Production 'Woman': J. M. Coetzee and Lewis Nkosi." *Current Writing* 2.1 (1990): 117–129.

Dovey, Teresa. *The Novels of J. M. Coetzee: Lacanian Allegories*. Craighall: A.D. Donker, 1988.

————. "Writing in the Middle Voice." *Essays on African Writing, 1: A Re-evaluation*. Ed. Abdulrazak Gurnah. Oxford: Heinemann, 1993. 56–69.

Driver, Dorothy. "*Drum* Magazine (1951–9) and the Spatial Configurations of Gender." *Text, Theory, Space: Land, Literature and History in South Africa and Australia*. Ed. Kate Darian-Smith, Liz Gunner, and Sarah Nuttall. London: Routledge, 1996. 231–242.

DuPlessis, Michael. "Bodies and Signs: Inscriptions of Femininity in John Coetzee and Wilma Stockenstrom." *Journal of Literary Studies/Tydskrif vir Literatuurwetenskap* 4.1 (1988): 118–128.

Durrant, Samuel. "Bearing Witness to Apartheid: J. M. Coetzee's Inconsolable Works of Mourning." *Contemporary Literature* 40.3 (1999): 430–463.

————. "The Limits of Empathy: Becoming Stupid in J. M. Coetzee's *Disgrace*." Unpublished Conference Paper. *J. M. Coetzee and the Ethics of Intellectual*

Practice: An International Conference. University of Warwick, Coventry. 27 Apr. 2002.

Eckstein, Barbara. "The Body, the Word, and the State: J. M. Coetzee's *Waiting for the Barbarians.*" *Novel: A Forum on Fiction* 22.2 (1989): 175–198.

Elphick, Richard. *Kraal and Castle: The Founding of White South Africa.* New Haven: Yale UP, 1977.

Fanon, Frantz. *The Wretched of the Earth.* New York: Grove Weidenfeld, 1963.

Farred, Grant. "Back to the Borderlines: Thinking Race *Disgrace*fully." *Scrutiny2: Issues in English Studies in Southern Africa* 7.1(2000): 16–19.

First, Ruth and Ann Scott. *Olive Schreiner.* New York: Schocken, 1980.

Fisher, Elizabeth. *Woman's Creation.* New York: McGraw Hill, 1979.

Folks, Jeffrey J. "Artist in the Interregnum: Nadine Gordimer's *July's People.*" *Critique: Studies in Contemporary Fiction* 39.2 (1998): 115–126.

Forster, E. M. *A Passage to India.* New York: Harcourt Brace, 1924.

Gaard, Greta. "Living Interconnections with Animals and Nature." *Ecofeminism.* Ed. Greta Gaard. Philadelphia: Temple UP, 1993. 1–12.

Gallagher, Susan Van Zanten. "Torture and the Novel: J. M. Coetzee's *Waiting for the Barbarians.*" *Contemporary Literature* 29.2 (1988): 277–285.

Gauthier, Marni. "The Intersection of the Postmodern and the Postcolonial in J. M. Coetzee's *Foe.*" *English Language Notes* 34.4 (1997): 52–71.

Glenn, Ian. "Game Hunting in *In the Heart of the Country.*" *Critical Perspectives on J. M. Coetzee.* Ed. Graham Huggan and Stephen Watson. New York: St. Martin's, 1996. 120–137.

Goldblatt, Patricia. "Finding a Voice for the Victimized." *Multicultural Review* 9.3 (2000): 40–47.

Goldner, Ellen J. "Other(ed) Ghosts: Gothicism and the Bonds of Reason in Melville, Chesnutt, and Morrison." *MELUS* 24.1 (1999): 59–83.

Goodman, David. *Fault Lines: Journeys into the New South Africa.* Berkeley: U of California P, 1999.

Gordimer, Nadine. *A Sport of Nature.* New York: Knopf, 1987.

———. *Burger's Daughter.* London: Penguin, 1979.

———. *The Conservationist.* London: Penguin, 1972.

———. *The Essential Gesture: Writing, Politics and Places.* Ed. Stephen Clingman. New York: Penguin, 1989.

———. *July's People.* New York: Penguin, 1982.

———. "Living in the Interregnum." *The Essential Gesture: Writing, Politics and Places.* Ed. Stephen Clingman. New York: Penguin, 1989. 261–284.

———. *The Pickup.* New York: Penguin, 2002.

———. "Writing and Being." Nobel Prize Lecture. *Nobel e-Museum.* 7 Dec. 1991. 23 Feb. 2004. <http://www.nobel.se/literature/laureates/1991/gordimer-lecture.html>.

Graham, Lucy. "'Yes, I am giving him up': Sacrificial Responsibility and Likeness with Dogs in J. M. Coetzee's Recent Fiction." *Scrutiny2: Issues in English Studies in Southern Africa* 7.1(2000): 4–15.

Gramsci, Antonio. *Selections from the Prison Notebooks of Antonio Gramsci.* Ed. and trans. Quintin Hoare and Geoffrey Nowell Smith. New York: International Publishers, 1971.

Green, Michael. *Novel Histories: Past, Present, and Future in South African Fiction.* Johannesburg: Witswatersrand UP, 1997.

Greenfield, Matthew. "Coetzee's *Foe* and Wittgenstien's *Philosophical Investigations:* Confession, Authority, and Private Languages." *Journal of Narrative Technique* 25.3 (1995): 23–37.

Gruen, Lori. "Dismantling Oppression: An Analysis of the Connection Between Women and Animals." *Ecofeminism.* Ed. Greta Gaard. Philadelphia: Temple UP, 1993. 60–90.

Hall, Barbara. "The Mutilated Tongue: Symbols of Communication in J. M. Coetzee's *Foe.*" *Unisa English Studies* 31.1 (1993): 16–22.

Haraway, Donna. *The Companion Species Manifesto: Dogs, People, and Significant Otherness.* Chicago: Prickly Paradigm Press, 2003.

Harding, Wendy. "The Two Faces of Empire in *Waiting for the Barbarians.*" *Q/W/E/R/T/Y: Arts, Litteratures, & Civilisations du Monde Anglophone* 2 (1992): 211–218.

Hardt, Michael and Antonio Negri. *Empire.* Cambridge: Harvard UP, 2000.

Head, Bessie. *A Question of Power.* London : Heinemann, 1974.

Head, Dominic. *J. M. Coetzee.* Cambridge: Cambridge UP, 1997.

———. *Nadine Gordimer.* Cambridge: Cambridge UP, 1994.

Heywood, Christopher. *A History of South African Literature.* Cambridge: Cambridge, UP, 2004.

Horrell, Geogina. "J. M. Coetzee's *Disgrace:* One Settler, One Bullet and the 'New South Africa.'" *Scrutiny2: Issues in English Studies in Southern Africa* 7.1(2000): 25–32.

Huggan, Graham. "Evolution and Entropy in J. M. Coetzee's *Age of Iron.*" *Critical Perspectives on J. M. Coetzee.* Ed. Graham Huggan and Stephen Watson. London: Macmillan, 1996. 191–212.

Ignatieff, Michael. Introduction. *Truth and Lies: Stories from the Truth and Reconciliation Commission in South Africa.* By Jillian Edelstein. New York: New York Press, 2002. 15–21.

Irigaray, Luce. "Another 'Cause'—Castration." *Feminisms: An Anthology of Literary Theory and Criticism.* Ed. Robyn R. Warhol and Diane Price Herndl. New Brunswick: Rutgers UP, 1993. 404–412.

Jacobson, Dan. *The Trap; and, A Dance in the Sun.* Harmondsworth: Penguin, 1968.

Jameson, Frederic. "Third World Literature in an Era of Multinational Capitalism." *Social Text* 15 (1986): 65–88.

Janes, Regina. "'Writing without Authority': J. M. Coetzee and His Fictions." *Salmagundi* 114–115 (1997): 103–121.

Kafka, Franz. "A Hunger Artist." *"The Metamorphosis," "The Penal Colony," and Other Stories.* New York: Schocken, 1995. 243–256.

————. *The Trial.* New York: Schocken, 1998.

Katrak, Ketu H. "Decolonizing Culture: Toward a Theory of Post-Colonial Women's Texts." *The Post-Colonial Studies Reader.* Ed. Bill Ashcroft, Gareth Griffiths, and Helen Tiffin. London: Routledge, 1995. 255–258.

Kawash, Samira. "Terrorists and Vampires: Fanon's Spectral Violence of Decolonization." *Frantz Fanon: Critical Perspectives.* Ed. Anthony C. Alessandrini. London: Routledge, 1999. 235–257.

Kerr, Douglas. "Three Ways of Going Wrong: Kipling, Conrad, and Coetzee." *Modern Language Review* 95.1 (2000): 18–27.

Kossew, Sue. "The Anxiety of Authorship: J. M. Coetzee's *The Master of Petersburg.*" *English in Africa* 23.1 (1996): 67–88.

————. "The Politics of Shame and Redemption in J. M. Coetzee's *Disgrace.*" *Research in African Literatures* 34.2(2003): 155–162.

————. "'Women's Words': A Reading of J. M. Coetzee's Women Narrators." *Span* 37.1 (1993): 12–23.

Lawlan, Rachel. "*The Master of Petersburg:* Confession and Double Thoughts in Coetzee and Dostoevsky." *Ariel: A Review of International English Literature* 29.2 (1998): 131–157.

Lazar, Karen. "Gordimer's Leap into the 90s: Gender and Politics in *'Jump' and Other Stories.*" *South African Feminisms: Writing, Theory, and Criticism, 1990–1994.* Ed. M. J. Daymond. New York: Garland, 1996. 281–300.

Lenta, Margaret. "Autrebiography: J. M. Coetzee's Boyhood and Youth." *English in Africa,* 30 .1 (2003): 157–169.

Levinas, Emmanuel. *Entre Nous.* New York: Columbia UP, 1998.

Lin, Lidan. "J. M. Coetzee and the Postcolonial Rhetoric of Simultaneity." *International Fiction Review* 28.1–2 (2001): 42–53.

Lloyd, David. *Nationalism and Minor Literature: James Clarence Mangan and the Emergence of Irish Cultural Nationalism.* Berkeley: U of California P, 1987.

Lockett, Cecily. "Feminism(s) and Writing in English in South Africa." *South African Feminisms: Writing, Theory, and Criticism, 1990–1994.* Ed. M. J. Daymond. New York: Garland, 1996. 3–26.

Lockhart, Alison. "The Politics of Gender and the Post-Colonial Context: Female Subjects, J. M. Coetzee and *In the Heart of the Country.*" *Inter Action* 3(1995): 152–159.

Ma, Sheng-Mei. "Mourning with the (as a) Jew: Metaphor, Ethnicity, and the Holocaust in Art Spiegelman's *Maus.*" *Studies in American Jewish Literature* 16 (1997): 115–129.

Macaskill, Brian. "Charting J. M. Coetzee's Middle Voice." *Contemporary Literature* 35.3 (1994): 441–475.

Magona, Sindiwe. *Mother to Mother.* Boston: Beacon, 1998.

Maher, Susan Naramore. "Confronting Authority: J. M. Coetzee's *Foe* and the Remaking of *Robinson Crusoe.*" *International Fiction Review*18.1 (1991): 34–40.

Marais, Michael. "Death and the Space of the Response to the Other." Unpublished Conference Paper. *J. M. Coetzee and the Ethics of Intellectual Practice: An International Conference.* University of Warwick, Coventry. 27 Apr. 2002.

————. "Literature and the Labour of Negation: J. M. Coetzee's *Life & Times of Michael K.*" Journal of Commonwealth Literature 36.1 (2001): 107–125.

————. "'Little Enough, Less than Little: Nothing': Ethics, Engagement, and Change in the Fiction of J. M. Coetzee." *Modern Fiction Studies* 46.1 (2000): 159–182.

————. "Places of Pigs: The Tension Between Implication and Transcendence in J. M. Coetzee's *Age of Iron.*" *Journal of Commonwealth Literature* 31.1 (1996): 83–95.

————. "The Possibility for Ethical Action: J. M. Coetzee's *Disgrace.*" Scrutiny2: *Issues in English Studies in Southern Africa* 5.1 (2000): 57–63.

————. "Writing with Eyes Shut: Ethics, Politics, and the Problem of the Other in the Fiction of J. M. Coetzee." *English in Africa* 25.1 (1998): 43–60.

Martin, Richard G. "Narrative, History, Ideology: A Study of *Waiting for the Barbarians* and *Burger's Daughter.*" *Ariel: A Review of International English Literature* 17.3 (1986): 3–21.

Maus, Derek. "Kneeling Before the Father's Wand: Violence, Eroticism and Paternalism in Thomas Pynchon's *V* and J. M. Coetzee's *Dusklands.*" *Journal of Literary Studies/Tydskrif vir Literatuurwetenskap* 15.1–2 (1999): 195–217.

May, Brian. "J. M. Coetzee and the Question of the Body." *Modern Fiction Studies* 47.2 (2001): 391–420.

McLean, Adam. *The Triple Goddess: An Exploration of the Archetypal Feminine.* Grand Rapids: Phanes, 1989.

Medeiros, Paulo. "Cannibalism and Starvation: The Parameters of Eating Disorders." *Disorderly Eaters: Texts in Self-Empowerment.* Ed. Lilian R. Furst and Peter W. Graham. University Park: Pennsylvania State UP, 1992. 1–27.

Meffan, James and Kim L. Worthington. "Ethics before Politics: J. M. Coetzee's *Disgrace.*" *Mapping the Ethical Turn: A Reader in Ethics, Culture, and Literary Theory.* Ed. Todd F. Davis and Kenneth Womack. Charlottesville: UP of Virginia, 2001. 131–150.

Merivale, Patricia. "Audible Palimpsests: Coetzee's Kafka." *Critical Perspectives on J. M. Coetzee.* Ed. Graham Huggan and Stephen Watson. London: MacMillan, 1996. 152–167.

Minh-Ha, Trinh T. "No Master Territories." *The Post-Colonial Studies Reader.* Ed. Bill Ashcroft, Gareth Griffiths, and Helen Tiffin. London: Routledge, 1995. 215–218.

Millett, Kate. *The Politics of Cruelty: An Essay on the Literature of Political Imprisonment.* New York: Norton, 1994.

Millin, Sarah Gertrude. *God's Stepchildren.* New York: Boni and Liveright, 1924.

Minz, Sidney W. *Sweetness and Power: The Place of Sugar in Modern History.* New York: Penguin, 1988.

Mitchell, Breon. "Kafka and the Hunger Artists." *Kafka and the Contemporary Critical Performance*. Ed. Alan Udoff. Bloomington: Indiana UP, 1987. 236–255.

Modisane, Bloke. *Blame Me on History*. New York: Dutton, 1963.

Mohanty, Chandra Talpade. "Under Western Eyes: Feminist Scholarship and Colonial Discourse." *Colonial Discourse and Postcolonial Theory, A Reader*. Eds. Patrick Williams and Laura Christman. New York: Columbia UP, 1994. 196–220.

Morphet, Tony. "Two Interviews with J. M. Coetzee, 1983 and 1987." *TriQuarterly* 68/69 (1987): 454–464.

Morgan, Peter. "*Foe*'s Defoe and La Jeune Nee: Establishing a Metaphorical Referent for the Elided Female Voice." *Critique: Studies in Contemporary Fiction* 35.2 (1994): 81–96.

Morrison, Toni. *Beloved*. New York: Plume, 1988.

Moses, Michael Valdez. "The Mark of Empire; Writing, History, and Torture in J. M. Coetzee's *Waiting for the Barbarians*." *Kenyon Review* 15.1 (1993): 115–127.

Naumann, Michel. "Coetzee's Children of the Earth and Language." *Commonwealth Essays and Studies* 15.1 (1992): 36–38.

Ndebele, Njabulo. *"Fools" and Other Stories*. London: Readers International, 1986.

Nkosi, Lewis. *Home and Exile*. London: Longmans, 1965.

Ohlson, Thomas and Stephen John Stedman. *The New is Not Yet Born: Conflict Resolution in Southern Africa*. Washington, D.C.: Brookings Institution, 1994.

Parkhurst, Carolyn. *The Dogs of Babel*. New York: Back Bay, 2004

Paton, Alan. *Cry, the Beloved Country*. New York: Scribner's, 1948.

Patterson, Charles. *Eternal Treblinka: Our Treatment of Animals and the Holocaust*. New York: Lantern, 2002.

Peires, J. B. *The Dead Will Arise: Nongqawuse and the Great Xhosa Cattle Killing Movement of 1856–1857*. Johannesburg: Ravan, 1989. 243–252.

Peterson, Anna L. *Being Human: Ethics, Environment, and Our Place in the World*. Berkeley: U of California P, 2001.

Peterson, Kirsten Holst. "An Elaborate Dead End? A Feminist Reading of J. M. Coetzee's *Foe*." *A Shaping of Connections*. Eds. Hena Maes-Jelinek, Kirsten Holst Peterson, and Anna Rutherford. Sydney: Dangaroo Press, 1989. 243–252.

Phillips, Caryl. "Life and Times of John C." *English in Africa* 25.1 (1998): 61–70.

Plaatje, Sol T. *Mhudi*. Johannesburg: Quagga Press, 1975.

Pollan, Michael. "The Unnatural Idea of Animal Rights." *New York Times Magazine* 10 Nov. 2002, sec. 6: 59–64, 100, 110–111.

Poyner, Jane. "Truth and Reconciliation in J. M. Coetzee's *Disgrace*." *Scrutiny2: Issues in English Studies in Southern Africa* 5.2 (2000): 67–77.

Probyn, Elspeth. *Carnal Appetites: FoodSexIdentities*. London: Routledge, 2000.

Renders, Luc. "J. M. Coetzee's *Michael K*: Starving in a Land of Plenty." *Literary Gastronomy*. Ed. David Bevan. Amsterdam: Rodopi, 1988. 95–102.

Rich, Paul. "Apartheid and the Decline of the Civilization Idea: An Essay on Nadine Gordimer's *July's People* and J. M. Coetzee's *Waiting for the Barbarians*." *Research in African Literatures* 15.3 (1984): 365–393.

Ringuette, Dana J. "Complicity and Consequences: Pluralism, Pragmatism, and the Practice of J. M. Coetzee." *Works and Days: Essays in the Socio-Historical Dimensions of Literature and the Arts* 10.2 (1992): 7–29.

Roberts, Sheila. "Cinderella's Mothers: J. M. Coetzee's *In the Heart of the Country.*" *English in Africa* 19.1 (1992): 21–33.

Rody, Caroline. "The Mad Colonial's Daughter's Revolt: J. M. Coetzee's *In the Heart of the Country.*" *South Atlantic Quarterly* 93.1 (1994): 157–180.

Rolleston, James. "'A Hunger Artist' as Allegory of Modernism." *Approaches to Teaching Kafka's Short Fiction.* Ed. Richard T. Gray. New York: MLA, 1995. 135–142.

Rose, Jacqueline. "Apathy and Accountabilty: South Africa's Truth and Reconciliation Commission." *Raritan* 21.4 (2002): 175–195.

Rotberg, Robert I. *Ending Autocracy, Enabling Democracy: The Tribulations of Southern Africa, 1960–2000.* Cambridge: World Peace Foundation, 2002.

Rushdie, Salman. "J. M. Coetzee's Heart of Darkness." Rev. of *Disgrace,* by J. M. Coetzee. *Boston Globe* 8 May 2000: A19.

Ryan, Pamela. "The Future of South African Feminism." *South African Feminisms: Writing, Theory, and Criticism, 1990–1994.* Ed. M. J. Daymond. New York: Garland, 1996. 31–43.

Sax, Boria. *The Mythological Zoo: An Encyclopedia of Animals in World Myth, Legend, and Literature.* Santa Barbara: ABC-CLIO, 2001.

Scarry, Elaine. *The Body in Pain: The Making and Unmaking of the World.* New York: Oxford UP, 1985.

Schofield, Mary Anne. *Masking and Unmasking the Female Mind: Disguising Romances in Feminine Fiction, 1713–1799.* Newark: U of Delaware P, 1990.

Schreiner, Olive. *Story of an African Farm.* New York: Crown, 1987.

Scott, Joanna. "Voice and Trajectory: an Interview with J. M. Coetzee." *Salmagundi* 114/115 (1997): 82–102.

Sevry, Jean. "Coetzee the Writer and the Writer of Autobiography." *Commonwealth Essays and Studies* 22.2 (2000): 13–24.

Shulevitz, Judith. "Author Tour." Rev. of *Elizabeth Costello,* by J. M. Coetzee. *New York Times Book Review* 26 Oct. 2003: 15–16.

Speigle, Marjorie. *The Dreaded Comparison: Human and Animal Slavery.* Philadelphia: New Society Publishers, 1988.

Spiegelman, Art. *Maus I: My Father Bleeds History.* New York: Pantheon, 1986.

Spivak, Gayatri. "Can the Subaltern Speak?" *Colonial Discourse and Post-Colonial Theory.* Ed. Patrick Williams and Laura Christman. New York: Columbia UP, 1994. 66–111.

Stephenson, Glennis. "Escaping the Camps: The Idea of Freedom in J. M. Coetzee's *Life & Times of Michael K.*" *Commonwealth Novel in English* 4.1 (1991): 77–88.

Strauss, Peter. "Coetzee's Idylls: The Ending of *In the Heart of the Country.*" *Momentum: On Recent South African Writing.* Ed. M. J. Daymond, J. U. Jacobs, and Margaret Lenta. Pietermaritzburg, South Africa: U of Natal P, 1992. 121–128.

Suleri, Sara. "Woman Skin Deep: Feminism and the Postcolonial Condition." *Colonial Discourse and Postcolonial Theory, A Reader.* Eds. Patrick Williams and Laura Christman. New York: Columbia UP, 1994. 244–256.

Susskind, Anne. "The Émigré." *The Bulletin.* 9 April 2001. 29 May 2003. <http://bulletin.ninemsn.com.au/bulletin.site.articleIDs/8BFC696B399A292 CA256ABD0048EDE4?open&ui=domPrint>.

Themba, Can. *The Will to Die.* Ed. Donald Stuart and Roy Holland. London: Heinemann, 1972.

Thurston, Mary Elizabeth. *The Lost History of the Canine Race: Our 15,00-Year Love Affair with Dogs.* Kansas City: Andrews & McMeel, 1996.

Van Niekerk, Marlene. *Triomph.* Trans. Leon de Kock. Woodstock: Overlook, 1994.

Viola, Andre. "'Two Mothers and No Father': J. M. Coetzee's *Boyhood.*" *Commonwealth Essays and Studies* 20.1 (1997): 96–99.

Virgil. *The Aeneid.* Trans. C. H. Sisson. Manchester: Carcanet Press Ltd., 1986.

Wachtel, Eleanor. "The Sympathetic Imagination: A Conversation with J. M. Coetzee." *Brick: A Literary Journal* 67.1 (2001): 37–47.

Wagner, Kathrine M. "'Dichter' and 'Dichtung': Susan Barton and the 'Truth' of Autobiography." *English Studies in Africa* 32.1 (1989): 1–11.

Watson, Stephen. "Colonialism in the Novels of J. M. Coetzee." *Critical Perspectives on J. M. Coetzee.* Ed. Graham Huggan and Stephen Watson. New York: St. Martin's, 1996. 13–36.

——. "The Writer and the Devil: J. M. Coetzee's *The Master of Petersburg.*" *New Contrast* 22.4 (1994): 47–61.

Wenzel, Jennifer. "Keys to the Labyrinth: Writing, Torture, and Coetzee's Barbarian Girl." *Tulsa Studies in Women's Literature* 15.1 (1996): 61–71.

Williams, Joy. *Ill Nature: Rants and Reflections on Humanity and Other Animals.* New York: Lyons Press, 2001.

——. *The Quick and the Dead.* New York: Knopf, 2000.

——. "Safariland." *Ill Nature: Rants and Reflections on Humanity and Other Animals.* New York: Lyons Press, 2001. 23–38.

Williams, R. D. "The Sixth Book of the *Aeneid.*" *Oxford Readings in Virgil's* Aeneid. Ed. S. J. Harrison. Oxford: Oxford UP, 1990. 191–207.

Wright, Derek. "Black Earth, White Myth: Coetzee's *Michael K.*" *Modern Fiction Studies* 38.2 (1992): 435–444.

Wright, Laura. "Minor Literature and 'The Skeleton of Sense': Anorexia, Franz Kafka's 'A Hunger Artist,' and J. M. Coetzee's *Life & Times of Michael K.*" *Journal of Commonwealth and Postcolonial Studies* 8.1 (2001):109–123.

Index